THE MOMMY MANIFESTO

THE MOMMY MANIFESTO

How to Use Our Power to Think Big, Break Limitations, and Achieve Success

KIM LAVINE

WILEY

John Wiley & Sons, Inc.

Published by John Wiley & Sons, Inc., Hoboken, New Jersey.
Published simultaneously in Canada.

For general information on our other products and services or for technical support, please contact our Customer Care Department within the United States at (800) 762-2974, outside the United States at (317) 572-3993 or fax (317) 572-4002.

Wiley also publishes its books in a variety of electronic formats. Some content that appears in print may not be available in electronic books. For more information about Wiley products, visit our web site at www.wiley.com.

Library of Congress-Cataloging-in-Publication Data:

Lavine, Kim.
  The mommy manifesto : how to use our power to think big, break limitations, and achieve success / by Kim Lavine.
     p.   cm.
  Includes index.
  ISBN 978-0-470-45845-7 (cloth)
  1. New business enterprises.   2. Women-owned business enterprises.
3. Businesswomen.   I. Title.
  HD62.5.L387 2009
  658.1'1082—dc22   2009019168

Printed in the United States of America.

10 9 8 7 6 5 4 3 2 1

To Stephanie Milanowski,
who taught me that there are no limits to what one
person can do to change one mind, one street, one
community, or our world.

Contents

Contents

IT'S A HISTORIC TIME

Let's take our place in history. Forget all the talk about doom and gloom. Everything is changing; don't confuse change with fear. Old institutions are failing, but in their place new and better ones are being created. Barriers to entry are falling in the world of business in an epic fashion everywhere I look. We're in the midst of major technological advances that will change our lives in the United States and around the world for the better. People will be empowered in unique and exciting ways through unprecedented access to information and communication as well as channels of distribution. Beyond the historic economic opportunity lie the social benefits that will come from giving over a billion people a voice along with the platform to communicate with each other in real time for purposes of commerce, social networking, or maybe even more important, issues of peace and sustainability. It is an event that has never been seen before in human history,

and women are poised to take their place as leaders on this world stage. This is the revolution's manifesto.
    Join me.

                                                Kim Lavine
                                                June 2009

Sign The Manifesto at www.mommymillionaire.com.

Acknowledgments

I would like to thank the following people, without whose talent, love, and support this book would not have been possible:

My friend Terry Cross, who's walked through the valley of the shadow of business with me, and who inspires me with his wisdom, passion, and generosity.

My friend Diane Reverand, the most fabulous person in New York and therefore the world, who challenges me to write my best, and to live my best with passion, enthusiasm, and authenticity.

My agent Kirsten Neuhaus, whose smart, passionate dedication to me and this book took us on incredible journeys from the east coast to the west.

My boys Dylan and Ryan, who continue to make me laugh, cry, and love in new and more profound ways every day, "with love forever."

Introduction

WHAT? ARE YOU KIDDING ME?

Forty-five years after the first women's revolution, women still only make up 3 percent of top CEOs, earn only 75 percent of wages of men for equivalent work, and are 40 percent more likely than men to be living in poverty. Elderly women in the United States are 60 percent more likely to be living in poverty than their male counterparts. And don't get me started on children! Nobody's suffering more in this culture than children, who, according to the Catholic Campaign for Human Development, represent 36 percent of all impoverished people in the United States. In single-parent households headed by a female, more than half of the children are living in poverty, five times the rate of married-couple families. Women with children are at the bottom of the food chain in this country, and it's getting worse. According to the Equal Employment Opportunity Commission, during 2007, workplace pregnancy discrimination charges surged to a record high level, up 14 percent from 2006. At the same time, sexual harassment filings increased for the first time since 2000, up 7 percent from the previous year.

NO WONDER WOMEN ARE STARTING BUSINESSES IN RECORD NUMBERS

Fed up with a corporate world that penalizes them for being both women and mothers, and gender inequities that are getting worse, women are beginning to take control of their financial destinies in record numbers by starting their own businesses. Not only are there more than 11 million women entrepreneurs in this country, making up 48 percent of all businesses, but women are starting businesses today at twice the rate of men. This isn't just a trend; it's a sea change. In fact, the forecasted growth of women-owned companies from 48 percent to 55 percent over the next 5 years is a powerful phenomenon that will rewrite the American cultural landscape, changing work and family life in revolutionary ways. This movement is simultaneously driving the creation of America's New Economy, while transforming social conventions in meaningful and momentous ways in the United States and around the world.

BUT IT'S ONLY JUST BEGINNING!

It's not just that these numbers are revolutionary. It's the social conditions behind them where the real revolution lies. According to a recent poll by Oprah of 15,000 working and stay-at-home moms, two-thirds of the working moms said they would quit work and stay home with their kids if they could. Among the stay-at-home moms, more than one-third wished they worked outside the home. Put this many women looking for a solution to a problem together with the technology of the twenty-first century, and the next women's revolution is born. But this time the revolution isn't a political revolution, it's an economic revolution. It's not just a woman's revolution—it's a family revolution. It's not even a technology revolution anymore; it's a communication revolution. In fact, the battle might already be over.

OBVIOUSLY, THINGS NEED TO CHANGE!

This next women's revolution, unlike the first women's revolution, isn't going to waste a minute trying to figure out how to fix the system. Forget about trying to fix the system. The system is broken. It's time to admit that it's unfixable by all conventional standards. The current system wasn't built for women or children. It's a simple practical matter of trying to fit a square peg into a round hole—it can't be done, and all the repeated attempts to make it fit are insane, defined as doing the same thing over and over again and expecting a different result. It's time for us to build another system, one that doesn't penalize us twice for being women and mothers, where women can achieve personal and professional fulfillment without compromising our need to be great moms.

IT'S THE ECONOMY, STUPID

While business people, political pundits, and economic experts are wringing their hands trying to figure out how to respond to an economy transforming under the pressures of global competition, credit markets gone awry, and an uncertain stock market, 30 million entrepreneurs led by women are busy creating tomorrow's wealth and employment opportunities today. Forget about a recession. The United States is in the midst of the largest entrepreneurial surge this country has ever seen. In 2006, a record number of Americans started companies, including women, college students, seniors, corporate refugees, and recent immigrants, who in 2005 started 25 percent more companies per capita than U.S. citizens. According to the Small Business Administration, more new companies were created in the last year few years than at the height of dot-com hysteria in the late nineties. Estimates by the SBA's Office of Advocacy estimates that there were 27.2 million small businesses in the United States in 2007, and early indications are that more people than ever are starting businesses in 2009 in response to massive corporate downsizing and layoffs. Put this together with an unprecedented growth in private equity, providing $20 billion a year for start-up businesses in angel capital alone, and you can see that the United States is a tinderbox full of money ready to explode.

BUT WAIT, IT GETS WORSE BEFORE IT GETS BETTER

Having given up on the dream of finding jobs that fulfill personal and career aspirations without compromising our need to be great moms, we bailed from the corporate world, only to find the same roadblocks in starting our own businesses. What we're discovering is that the inequity doesn't end in the workplace. The inequity extends to equity itself, or to be more specific, to private equity, or the money that is available as capital to start businesses in the United States. Despite the fact that women own 48 percent of all businesses in this country, only

4 percent of the available $20 billion in angel capital goes to fund women-owned companies every year. With access to capital a major contributing factor to starting and growing a business, it's no wonder that only 3 percent of all woman-owned businesses have revenues of one million dollars or more every year. What?! Is that fair? Apparently not, because the Kauffman Foundation—the nation's premiere entrepreneurial organization—just issued a mandate to investors to invest in woman-owned businesses. There's never been a better time in history for women to access capital!

THIS IS YOUR WAKE-UP CALL

The new breed of women entrepreneurs in search of an answer to a broken system is using the tools of new technology to create a New Economy. Never before has it been more true that necessity is the mother of invention. Or in this case, mothers are the necessity to invention. Take it from somebody on the front lines: Everything in the world of business is up for grabs. The book is being rewritten daily on what the new wealth opportunities of tomorrow are. The creation, distribution, and control of money-making ideas is leaving the hands of the few and transferring to the hands of the many in new and fundamentally different ways every day. You used to have to build railroads to become a millionaire. Now, musicians are taking their products direct to consumers on the Internet. Manufacturers are reaching out to buyers across the world for pennies. Millions will watch one video on YouTube in just one day. The people who made their money just 10 years ago are wondering how to do it again today in a totally new marketplace. Everything is different. Everything is changing. Despite the best efforts of those few who controlled so much of our access to opportunity before, the toothpaste is out of the tube, and no matter how hard they try, they can't put it back in the way it was.

WHAT'S HOLDING YOU BACK?

Today's business titans of the old economy are afraid of us and are simultaneously looking to us to show them the way to new money-making opportunities. They're counting on us not realizing that the only thing separating us from them is our self-doubt, while they try to figure out how to keep the genie in the bottle or opportunity in the hands of the few. They're counting on women to not recognize the power they have to dramatically affect this precarious situation. As in the heyday of the dotcom era in the late 90s, people with money and power are competing to invest in anyone with an idea and a roadmap to take them forward into this brave new world. For the first time in history, you may not need that investment.

IN TIMES OF GREAT PERIL, COMES GREAT OPPORTUNITY

Nobody said this was going to be easy. Nobody said that recreating the United States' economy to survive the future and create equity for women, while simultaneously transforming social conventions in meaningful and momentous ways both in this country and around the world, wasn't going to involve some kind of struggle or sacrifice. But what's the alternative? Things aren't getting better for us as women, they're getting worse. Maintaining the status quo is not an option—change is the only option. No more waiting around for society to give us the respect we deserve. It's time for us to take it! If we were men, we would be knocking down doors to get it.

ALL GREAT JOURNEYS ARE BEGUN ON THE STRENGTH OF ONE INDIVIDUAL AND HIS FAITH

So what's stopping us from knocking down doors? What's stopping us from raising private equity to start and grow our record number of businesses? What's stopping us after we raise start-up capital from taking our companies to over a million dollars in revenues a year? Is it just going to take more women to have faith? Do we just need a dream? A hero? A vision? Or is it a simple matter of confidence? Do we need to turn off the internal dialog telling us we can't do it and believe in ourselves instead? What is the internal dialog in women's heads nowadays anyway, and who's programming it? Maybe we need to replace "lose weight, be pretty, lose weight, be pretty, lose weight," with "kick butt, knock down doors, stand up for ourselves, be smart, and take what's ours." Maybe we should figure out what we need to do to get our fair share and program that in instead.

ARE SOME OF US OUR OWN WORST ENEMIES?

Isn't it time we stopped the negative self-talk that tells us we're too fat, our house isn't clean or well decorated enough, that our car isn't big enough, our husband's job not prestigious enough? There are a hundred books out there telling women about all the stupid mistakes we make to mess up our lives, our marriages, our jobs, our diets, our money. At every supermarket checkout there are a hundred magazines telling us to be skinnier, prettier, richer, sexier, better dressed, with perfect homes and better cooking skills. Where are the books and magazines telling us we're already skinny and pretty enough? Where are the books and magazines telling us how to be richer, better dressed, with better decorated homes by owning our own businesses and economic futures? Where are the books that tell us that our measure of success as mothers is not how clean and well-decorated our houses are, but how happy our kids are? Is there even one book directed at men that gives them the same messages of self-contempt for every one hundred books for women? Most of these authors are women themselves, who've made lucrative careers from telling women on TV and radio that they're not good enough, smart enough, nor thin enough, or that they don't keep their houses clean enough to approach some unattainable ideal. Enough with telling women they're not good enough! I'm here to tell you are and that you can achieve any dream you want, if only you make up your mind to do so. This world does not need one more book or magazine or voice telling women they don't measure up just so that somebody can make a profit selling them diet pills, cleaning supplies, wrinkle cream, or even books.

THE NEXT SHOE IS ABOUT TO DROP

All these constant messages have created a false god of consumerism that women have come to worship, and by which they've come to value themselves. It's an empty, unforgiving god that measures a woman's value by clothes, shoes, decorated houses, and fancy cars instead of the achievement of personal or professional hopes, dreams, and aspirations. Don't get me wrong—I'm not above great shoes! I love fabulous shoes just as much as the next girl, but what's really exciting is wearing drop-dead shoes to my own company's board meeting, for which I'm the chairman, or even to my kids' Christmas pageant at school in the middle of a workday, because I'm the boss, and I don't have to feel guilty about it or ask anyone's permission to go. What's ironic is that women have been driven into out-of-control consumerism as the definitive measure of our success, while we own the very market on consumerism! How can we control something so unilaterally and absolutely, yet be driven by the capricious whims created by arbitrary cultural arbiters, whose job it is to make us feel we're too fat, have too many wrinkles and a less-than-perfect house, all in an attempt to sell us products to power the consumer market that we control?

LET'S BE OUR OWN CULTURAL ARBITERS

Let's do something really revolutionary. Let's take control of the channels of distribution, not only for consumer products, but for all the information that enters the marketplace telling women the ideals to which they should aspire. This is happening as you read this, thanks to innovations in the way we communicate. For the first time in history, women all over the United States and even the world are talking to each other on the Web, tearing down the culture of the past and recreating the culture they want, complete with new values that aren't designed to make them feel empty, or inadequate, or undervalued, in order to sell them something. Imagine being in control of giving ourselves daily messages of powerful affirmation. Imagine a world where our values are no longer sold to us, but we're the ones doing the selling. We need a new declaration of lifestyle that focuses on having it all. This is it!

YOU CAN HAVE IT ALL

Another myth holding us back is the myth that women can't have it all. By that I mean, we can't have satisfying and rewarding professional lives *and* be great moms at the same time. The often quoted mantra of the day is "women can have it all, just not at the same time." Wrong! This is just another myth to keep us from trying or make us feel guilty—guilty for having a job, guilty for not having a job, guilty for not having a good enough job, guilty for sacrificing our career to stay home with kids, guilty for sacrificing staying home with kids for our career. Enough with the guilt already! For that matter, enough with the jobs. Today's women are shouldering so much guilt, it's amazing they can even get out of bed in the morning. This includes guilt about our kids, guilt about that pile of laundry we can't lick, guilt about that missed workout, guilt about that missed opportunity to follow a dream. The myth that women can't have it all at the same time is especially pernicious. It seems to make sense in the world we're leaving behind, but in the world we are on the cusp of creating, where we take control of our own financial destinies by starting our own businesses, nothing could be further from the truth. Again, the number one propagators of this myth are women! Let's come right out and admit it right up front: Sometimes we're our own worst enemies. It only makes sense that this would be the case in a world in which success for women is scarce, a precious commodity we not only have to compete with men for but compete with each other for. The truth is, in the new world we're creating, there's enough success for everyone to go around. Once we don't have to compete for limited job opportunities, instead taking control of our own financial destinies by becoming our own bosses, we can do away with the myths, the jealousy, the guilt, and the emptiness—along with the inequity, discrimination, and the lousy pay.

IT'S NO WONDER

It's no wonder women find it tough to succeed when they bring all this baggage to the brink of opportunity and have to compete with men who don't have the same self-defeating attitude programmed into them. Speaking in a vernacular I've learned from years in the male-dominated world of business, getting to the top demands such incredible fortitude, such Herculean nerve, such *balls out, balls-to-the-wall, ball-busting, brass balls* confidence that even a moment's hesitation in the race to each day's finish line can result in failure. (Just for a minute, try to think of any analogies to boobs that symbolize strength or courage, or that you could even say aloud in a boardroom, where I've heard all these male images spouted.) Years into my own journey on the roller-coaster ride that is entrepreneurship, I was told by my then-chairman of the board, a former Wall Street titan and founding investor in Google, Inktomi, and PayPal to name a few, that I had only one thing to thank for my success: balls, or in other words, the gall to stand up for myself and demand what was mine. That was it—the secret in a nutshell. In this world having balls and being a woman can just as easily be confused with being a bitch. It's time to redefine that, too.

REDEFINING SUCCESS

Again, I'm not talking about a stinking job, or a seat in some megalomaniac's boardroom, where you work 80 hours a week making someone else's dream happen. I'm not talking about being a prisoner in a house where you measure your success by how clean and well-decorated it is. I'm not talking about determining your self worth by the measure of status your husband achieves, as you work to support him in the pursuit of his career or dreams. I'm talking about developing the kind of confidence it takes to say "screw this job thing and this house-cleaning thing" while you pull yourself up by the bootstraps, push away adversity, face down doubt, get your business plan torn up and thrown in your face, and close a million-dollar deal with world-class people working for you. I'm talking about learning to value ideas and passion over degrees and job titles, of having the courage to believe in your dreams and go after them while simultaneously teaching your kids to be in control of their own financial destinies by becoming entrepreneurs themselves. I'm talking about filling in that aching black hole of being away from your kids, not by choice but because of a job. I'm talking about being able to watch them grow, understanding that everything they do, say, mess up, or break, is given to you as a special gift from God to make you laugh, cry, and love in new and more profound ways every day. These are the skills women need! Not thinner thighs in 30 days. Not the reduced appearance of fine lines and wrinkles. Not the dream of an immaculate house, the attainment of which is shattered the moment kids and life enter the picture.

YOU'RE FABULOUS—NOW OWN IT!

We're the architects of this New Economy. It's time for us to take our share! Instead of waiting for jobs or money or freedom to be handed to you, take your place at the table, embark upon the journey of following a dream, and create tomorrow's wealth and employment opportunities today. Don't call us feminists, call us boss! It's a new time and a new generation of women, and this is a new message of empowerment. We're not asking for a job. This is a new way of living, and we're bringing our kids with us this time. Consider this a cannonball fired across your bow.

CHAPTER 1

How to Start a Revolution

Quick. Picture a typical mom. What do you see?

Moms have become an analogy for the powerless, the anti-sexy, the timid underdog. More often than not they're seen as harried, wearing bad jeans, in need of a makeover, or some kind of life transformation that drags them out of their homes into some job for a day, where they're bossed around, told what to do, and made to feel generally inadequate in order to reveal to them all the things they're missing by sacrificing their lives to take care of those pesky kids. That is, unless we're talking about commercials, where moms are shown to be all bright and shiny, ensconced in an immaculate kitchen, or bathroom, or something else they're furiously trying to keep bright and shiny.

Let's face it, a mom is an image nobody aspires to—an image more likely than not to be the subject of ridicule. The image of a mom has become so maligned that I know women who won't even admit to being mothers

1

on job interviews, fearing they won't be hired because they have children. Hey, I've been there. Going to sleep with baby puke on your shoulder, waking up with baby puke on your shoulder, taking showers between cartoons, breastfeeding babies all day while watching commercials telling you you'd better get around to scrubbing that toilet again and disinfecting your entire house of all possible germs in the universe. That, or watching reruns of *Teletubbies*, or the cartoon *du jour* all day, or inane talk shows where—aside from celebrities—only those women willing to reveal their innermost embarrassing secrets and shortcomings are deemed interesting enough to be on TV shows that exploit their misery. Can you believe these ordinary puke-stained, baby-balancing, toddler-chasing moms are the women who are creating and leading the revolution?

MOM IS THE NEW SEXY

Why? Because power is sexy, and the new moms are powerful. That's right, you're powerful, and you don't even know it yet! Your power might even be scary! In fact, it is threatening to certain people, who are hoping you don't figure out how powerful you have become, until they figure out a way to continue to sell you the insecurity that keeps you in your place. In the cultural universe, the planets have aligned, opening a pathway to power and possibility for women, particularly mommies, unlike anything seen previously in history. Is it really possible that the ultimate underdog and perhaps the most marginalized demographic in American society—ironically made up of 38 million women with children—is suddenly the most powerful group on earth? You'd better believe it!

THIS ISN'T YOUR MOTHER'S MOTHER ANYMORE

Forget about soccer moms. Forget about millennium moms, and alpha moms, too. Today's moms are Manifesto Moms, defying any narrow categorization except that they're uniquely plugged into technology, particularly technology that enables communication such as my smartphone, which has become a natural extension of my own right hand. This new definition of moms includes everybody, not just those with college degrees, high household incomes, big SUVs, accomplished careers, or kids in sports. Even if you've never spent a day in college and find yourself working at Wal-Mart and scraping together enough money to buy toilet paper and macaroni and cheese for your family, you still have the power. If you can turn on a computer and surf the Web for free at the library, that's where power lies. It's the ordinary mom's ability to use new communication tools to shape and influence opinion that is historic, and radical, and transforming.

IT'S A COMMUNICATION REVOLUTION, STUPID

What makes Manifesto Moms special—and dangerous to the status quo—is their adeptness in using technology to communicate in new and powerful ways. Manifesto Moms surf the Web an average of an hour and a half a day—that's more than some of them spend watching TV—and that number is increasing daily. Manifesto Moms are not just passively surfing the Web looking for content created by the usual suspects; they're creating the content that they can't find anywhere else. They're building their own online communities, writing their own blogs, making their own videos, capturing their own personal and dramatic stories, most of which have never been told before by any conventional media outlet, creating infinitely more fascinating, riveting, real and moving stories than anyone could make up. Real stories, by real women—imagine that! And guess what? They're not like anything you see on TV. Instead, these stories are of fulfilling hopes, dreams, and aspirations, of husbands losing their jobs, of struggles with special needs children, of newly divorced women confronting new responsibility that centers on them alone, of emptiness that neither consumerism nor a sparkling house can fill. These stories are being told and being read by women all over the world, who are discovering that whether they live in the United States, in England, in France, Denmark, Korea, India, or China, they are all in pursuit of the same thing: respect, freedom, the opportunity to find personal or professional fulfillment without compromising their maternal roles, and a society and a workplace that doesn't penalize them for being women. Most of these stories, revelations, and affirmations are centered on women who are saying "enough is enough," and "screw this job thing," who are instead taking control of their financial destinies by starting their own businesses, chasing dreams for personal and professional fulfillment from their kitchen tables, in between making peanut butter-and-jelly sandwiches for their kids.

THERE ISN'T ENOUGH MONEY IN THE WORLD TO BUY THIS

It's not just the Web. This communication involves cell phones, e-mail, text messages, BlackBerries, Pres, and iPhones. It's videos sent from smartphones and uploaded to YouTube where they're watched by millions in just hours. It's 255 million wireless subscribers, or 85 percent of the entire U.S. population, who will soon have the added ability to get the same content they're searching out or creating on the Web on their cell phones, whether they're at the park, at a job, at a PTA meeting, on the sideline of their child's soccer game, or hiding behind a bathroom door for a few minutes of peace while toddlers pound for their attention on the other side. But it's 10 times bigger than this—it's 3 billion wireless handsets in use across the world and another 500 million being added every year. Just like that, gone is the isolation that kept these mommies voiceless, powerless, and lonely. Instead, women are trading in their victim status as media consumers for ruling status as media creators. Women are talking; women with opinions, women shaping opinions, women finding their voices. As women find their voice in each other, they have yet to perceive how powerful it is. I'm here to tell them.

WHAT'S THE BIG DEAL?

The revolutionary phenomenon is this: There are infinite channels of worldwide distribution with immediate delivery, at almost no cost. Can you believe it? Is that revolutionary enough for you? Women can communicate with each other in real time, disseminating ideas, shaping opinion, redefining lifestyle, making their own media, and creating worldwide influence. Giving 38 million women with children a voice? And that's just in the United States. When you add in the number of women with children around the world, the influence—and power—of women becomes exponential. It's a new world, and in this world ideas are

5

currency. They can become powerful overnight, but wait, there's more! As mind-blowingly powerful as that is, it's not even where the real power lies!

CONTENT IS KING AND CONTACT IS QUEEN

In the world of new media, content is still king, but contact comes in a close second as queen. Especially for mommies, who have historically struggled with the isolation that goes along with being stuck as the only adult in a house, consumed with the incredibly demanding job of raising good kids while looking at the world as if from the outside in. What the heck is new media and what is content? New media refers to the new computerized, digital technologies that allow you to watch, read and communicate online, on the Web, or on your smartphone. Content refers to the information in whatever form—audio, video, printed words and so on—communicated via the new media. Unlike TV, new media content is usually something you seek out, instead of waiting for it to be delivered to you. Once you find it, you can watch it whenever and wherever you'd like, as many times as you like. New media content is the toothpaste that has already come out of the tube. It's messy and free and uncensored, made by mommies and kids with skateboards, and anyone else with a video camera or even a phone. With new media, ideas find immediate expression and delivery into the marketplace. The contact part of the equation comes in when we receive those ideas and embrace them. Anybody can put ideas into the marketplace nowadays. Millions of women have their own blogs where they create their own special form of content. There's lots of great undiscovered content

How to Start a Revolution

all over the Web. The creation of content isn't remarkable anymore, though remarkable content is still rare and incredibly valuable, making it king. The ability to connect with others through that content is what is remarkable, and a lot of people unfortunately are using other people's remarkable content right now to make those connections for their own profit. The ability to reach out and create a social network or international community around unique and original content is where the real power is found. It's not content that makes Google worth just under $200 billion. With that valuation you would think that Google owns all the content it points to all over the Web, but, of course, that just isn't the case. It's not content that turned YouTube founders into billionaires overnight. It's *contact* that makes both these companies so valuable, the ability to use other people's content to not only connect millions of people across the world in seconds, but simultaneously to sell advertising, and eventually products to those same millions.

JUST ONE MORE BALLS ANALOGY

There's so much money to be had in new media—or the revolutionary ability to create both content and contact—that Sumner Redstone, an old media titan and majority stockholder in media giant Viacom, reportedly bragged about it, claiming to shareholders that "they would all be dipping their balls in gold" as a result of the money they were going to make. I wonder where that left ball-less women shareholders? This new form of contact is powered by innovative ideas. The more innovative the ideas, the more powerful and influential the contact attached to it is. These ideas are creating revolutionary new trends across the world at record speed. The winners in this new world are going to be those people who have innovative ideas. Technology and the contact creators are just the machine, but it's content that makes the machine work. The real opportunities for money and power in the new media world include you, working out of your home while helping kids with homework, pushing them on swings, or driving them to their soccer games.

AND NOW FOR SOMETHING COMPLETELY REVOLUTIONARY

Besides telling their own stories, these Manifesto Moms are becoming cultural arbiters, flexing new muscles in the influence department, shaping buying decisions when even the most expensive Madison Avenue ad agency with the biggest budget cannot. In fact, Madison Avenue ad agencies are courting these new plugged-in Manifesto Moms and worrying about them at the same time, understanding their social influence and knowing how important contact is in creating connection with consumers, they're seeking their praise. They know they can't keep us down on the farm anymore, watching the content they put on broadcast TV, confident that our butts will be in chairs for specific hours on a regular weekly basis. Sure, maybe Manifesto Moms will record their favorite programs on their DVRs, but it's all but certain that we'll fast-forward through the commercials, something called time shifting. Why? Because we're early adopters—a phrase that describes those people who embrace new technology before most other people do. Besides young men, the only other large group of early adopters are women in the 18- to 34-year-old age group—or mommies! Who's got a greater need to time shift than mommies? In fact, women lead even young men in time shifting and web surfing. Getting the content we want to watch at the time we want to watch it—especially during that midnight feeding or after the kids have gone to bed or even on the sideline of our kids' soccer game on our smartphones—is what it's all about!

A WORD TO THE WISE

Where is all this new media money coming from? Advertising to Manifesto Moms, that's where. If we're not getting our media on broadcast TV, and if we are fast-forwarding through commercials, how are advertisers going to connect with us? Why is it important that advertisers connect with us anyway? Because we're the most powerful consumers on earth—that's why! Women are not only chief purchasing officers for their families and households, they are the single most important factor in the U.S. economy. It's estimated that women in the United States control 85 percent of consumer spending, or $8.5 trillion annually. That's 75 percent of this country's economy! When consumer purchases account for 75 percent of this country's economic activity, just the mention of the word "recession" can bring Wall Street to its knees in fear that it will become a self-fulfilling prophecy. In a culture in which success is so often measured by the outward display of conspicuous consumption, consumer confidence is everything, and yet it is as fickle as dandelion down on the wind. It's time for the United States' 38 million women with children to recognize their power to control the country's economy—and its future. And as America goes, so goes the world.

CHAPTER 2

Shock and Awe

"Woman is the nigger of the world."
—Yoko Ono

WOMEN ARE GOING BACKWARD!

Here's the *new* news. Wake up and smell the coffee! Women are not gaining equity on gender issues across the board—in some cases *they're going backward!*

SEXISM—THE LAST ACCEPTABLE FORM OF BIGOTRY

Things are not only getting worse for women, they're getting worse at the same time that the opportunities of the New Economy are being created, accelerating men into the fast lane of what may be one of the most epic periods of economic transformation in our country's history—if not the world's. If we don't make our voices heard now and take our rightful places in this new economic world order, we're going to be left behind in a way that we may not recover from for decades. That's not just bad for us; that's bad for the world at this critical point in history, as I'm going to show you. We need to empower ourselves with all the skills, knowledge, and tools that men are using to stake out this new frontier, before they claim it all as theirs again, which they're busy doing! Every day we wait is a day too late!

HOLD YOUR ANGER TO THE END

Facts are going to come at you quickly now. Hold your anger for the end. Women make up 51 percent of the population, but consider the following statistics.

GOVERNMENT

- In the United States Congress, only 87 of the 535 members—or 16.3 percent—are women.
- In the United States Senate women hold only 16 out of 100 seats, or 16 percent.
- In the United States House of Representatives, 71 of the 435 available seats are held by women or 16.3 percent.
- There are currently 8 women governors in the United States. You guessed it: 16 percent.

I realized that sexism was the last acceptable form of bigotry during this last presidential race when I saw the personal low blows Hillary Clinton was taking from not just the peanut gallery but the legitimate mainstream press. Sure, I wasn't at all surprised to hear Rush Limbaugh rhetorically ask if this country was ready to "watch a woman age in the White House." Chris Matthews, already known for his provocative commentary, called Hillary a "she-devil" and said she had only gotten where she is because her husband had "messed around." But I remember feeling disbelief and revulsion hearing Tucker Carlson of MSNBC say, "Every time I hear Hillary Clinton speak, I involuntarily cross my legs." Where was the public outrage, or for that matter, the rebuke of Carlson by his bosses at MSNBC for making such a reprehensible, sexist statement? Even candidate Obama wouldn't acknowledge the problem in public, saying through Representative Debbie Wasserman Schultz, Democrat of Florida, that he had no specific plans to address issues of sexism in a speech because he already "incorporates themes of discrimination as a societal problem." On the political front, only Howard Dean, chairman of the Democratic National Committee, was willing to publicly admit that "the media took a very sexist approach to Senator Clinton's campaign," calling it "appalling," and observing that she "got treated the way a lot of women got treated their whole lives." The only media person courageous enough to take a public stand was Katie Couric, who attracted her own share of criticism when she became the first solo woman anchor of an evening news show. Posting a video on the CBS web site criticizing Clinton's treatment, she called out those who were willing to passively accept sexism in silence.

From where I stood, all I saw was a bunch of indignant e-mails shuffled around between my female friends and business associates in the New York intelligentsia, any of whom could have just as easily called up the president of

NBC to demand an apology but settled for complaining in private instead. Can you imagine the firestorm that would have ensued if a mainstream news anchor made similar comments regarding President Obama's sexual appeal, or more explosively, race? Are we, including the most successful and well-connected women I know in New York, afraid to publicly call foul when we see it, for fear of being branded with that most notorious, stigmatized, reviled, and mocked title in contemporary culture: *feminist?*

"Of my two handicaps, being female put more obstacles in my path than being black."
—Shirley Chisholm

WALL STREET

- None of the leading Wall Street banks—Goldman Sachs, the combined Bank of America and Merrill Lynch, JPMorgan Chase, Citigroup, UBS, Credit Suisse, or Morgan Stanley—has a single woman in any of the top three jobs. That's according to a story by Anita Raghavan in *Forbes*, titled "Terminated: Why the Women of Wall Street Are Disappearing," published in March of 2009.

It's extremely difficult to find any specific data about women on Wall Street, but according to this same story in *Forbes*, women are not only significantly underrepresented, they are also disproportionately being singled out for layoffs during this current economic downturn, not only in the lower ranks but at the highest executive levels, too. This last year has seen the departure of three of the street's most prominent female executives in the shake-out from an uncertain financial climate where it seems only the men survive; Zoe Cruz, former co-president of Morgan Stanley; Sallie Krawcheck, chairman and CEO of Citigroup's Global Wealth Management division; and Erin Callan, Lehman Brothers Holdings' chief financial officer, have all lost their jobs

At the 2009 World Economic Forum in Davos, Switzerland, only 6 of the 80 world economic leaders in attendance were women, and Neelie Kroes, the European commissioner for competition, was quoted in "Talking Banks and Sex," in the *New York Times* on January 31, 2009, by Katrin Bennhold, saying she was "absolutely convinced" that testosterone-driven egos were one of the reasons the financial system went into crisis. In the same story, Mari Pangestu, the Indonesian Trade minister, reported that research in her country demonstrated that when it came to money, women were "more prudent and less corrupt." Even Harvard economist Kenneth Rogoff agreed that we wouldn't be in the economic mess we're in if we had "more gender diversity in the finance sector."

"The current crisis gives us the opportunity to insert gender into the rewriting of the rules," says Nadereh Chamlou, a senior adviser at the World Bank. "We need more women at the table."

There's so much fear and secrecy in this last old boy's bastion of power that just about every woman who does have a job on Wall Street is afraid to talk about discrimination, or worse yet, sue, for fear of becoming permanently exiled from her ability to make a living in this very insular world. In my own travels across this country I've heard horror stories from some of the women who worked on Wall Street, such as being ostracized or dismissed upon returning from maternity leave, or unimaginably worse, investment banking bosses suggesting abortions to their pregnant staff. Barack Obama's appointment of a woman, Mary Schapiro, to head up the Securities and Exchange Commission, an independent U.S. government agency established by Congress in 1934 to police and regulate the securities industry and Wall Street, may be an important step in helping women gain equal access to opportunity in the financial industry. Until then, I'm still waiting to see the male version of CNBC's amazingly beautiful "Money Honey" Maria Bartiromo delivering mind-blowingly smart business analysis and news from the Street. But I guess looks aren't a prerequisite to getting an on-air job as a financial expert if you're a man.

PRIVATE EQUITY

- Despite owning 48 percent of all businesses in the United States, women still only receive an average of 4 percent of private equity money each year to start and grow their businesses.
- As a result, because of a lack of access to capital, only 3 percent of women-owned businesses in the United States have annual revenues of a million dollars or more.

Let me remind you to hold your anger to the end. In my experience, whenever I drop this statistic, whether it's on TV, in a keynote speech, or even at dinner in the governor's residence, nothing elicits more shock and indignation than this telling fact. Try this at home: Ask one of your friends to take a guess what percentage of the total amount of private equity available every year the 11 million women-owned businesses successfully raise. See? Told you!

What is private equity exactly? It's the money people use to start and grow businesses. It generally comes in two forms: venture capital (VC) and angel capital. Both types comprise private investors regulated by the Securities and Exchange Commission. Venture capital is generally out-of-reach for most start-up and even mid-stage businesses, with a typical minimum investment of $2 million. Angel capital, on the other hand, is a rather new phenomenon, which happens to be experiencing a 20 percent annual growth rate, providing money at an early or first-stage round for emerging companies, with a much lower investment threshold and a more patient exit strategy. Angel investors are usually high-net-worth individuals who come together in their local communities to stimulate economic growth and development through investments in local businesses. Angel investors didn't get rich by giving away money, and they'll gladly eat you for breakfast if you show them one iota of weakness, so don't confuse them with anything remotely beneficent or holy. I successfully raised angel capital while simultaneously recruiting world-class management to work for my company, and I painstakingly detail the incredible journey of how to do it in my first book, *Mommy Millionaire*.

The best information regarding angel investment in women-owned companies comes courtesy of the Ewing Marion Kauffman Foundation, which issued a report on this trend in 2007, along with a mandate to angels to invest in women-owned businesses. It's not clearly understood why the percentage of private equity invested in women-owned businesses is so low at 4 percent, especially when it comes to angel capital. New research by the Center for Venture Research at the University of New Hampshire, suggests that women seek angel financing at much lower rates than men, but when they do, they have an equal probability of receiving investment capital. According to the Center for Women's Business Research, the investment opportunity in women-owned businesses is a virtually untapped market. In response to this, several angel funds have been created nationwide, along with LFE, a venture capital fund, targeting investment in women-led companies. One of these is the Sofia Fund, headquartered in Minneapolis. Cathy Connett, an investor in Sofia and chairwoman of the fund makes no bones about it: "This is not a charity. We are trying to facilitate women's access to money but [the bottom line is] we want to make money. It's somewhat of an old-boy network ... and women entrepreneurs aren't necessarily connected into that network" "Angel Fund Focuses on Women's Firms: Sofia Aims to Close Seed-Money Gap," Julie Forster, *Knight Ridder Tribune Business News*, Washington, March 29, 2006.

The short story is, it's a time of incredible opportunity for women to raise capital to start and grow their businesses. Not only is there a lot of money available, but there's a deliberate attempt by the people who matter to call out investors who aren't investing equally in women-owned businesses. So get my first book and get out there and push your business plan in front of every angel investor you can find both online and off. Don't deny yourself the unique and unparalleled opportunity of having your business plan ripped up and thrown in your face, which actually happened to me just months before I successfully closed my angel deal. Stand up for yourself, take some knocks, make lots of pitches, take 'em to the mat, and close some deals. Just remember, be careful out there, and never let them see you sweat.

CORPORATE

- Only 2.6 percent of Fortune 500 companies have women CEOs, according to an annual examination by *USA Today*.
- A 2008 survey of CEO pay by the Corporate Library found that female CEOs made 85 percent of what male CEOs made, but that percentage changes dramatically when bonuses, which make up a significant portion of executive compensation, are added in.

We've all heard of the glass ceiling, a phrase used to describe the invisible barrier women encounter on their way up the corporate ladder to success. Despite the fact that women constitute 44 percent of the workforce nationally, less than 3 percent of the top positions in the United States' biggest companies are held by women. Though the salary gap between women and men across the employment spectrum is just over 21 percent, the pay discrepancy at the top between women and men is worse, according to U.S. Department of Labor statistics. While the 100 top-earning women in corporate America last year earned an average of $3 million, their male counterparts made on average a whopping $18 million. According to a report by Judith H. Dobrzynski in *Forbes* magazine, titled "The Highest-Paid Women In Corporate America," published September 10, 2008, the median salary for the chief executives of the 100 largest U.S. companies—all men—is about twice the median salary of the 100 highest-paid women. This pay discrepancy is linked most directly to performance bonuses awarded on top of salary; according to a recent study by the University of Cambridge, some link testosterone levels to a willingness to take the risks that bring in the big bonuses, at least in terms of Wall Street traders. With testosterone already being blamed for much of Wall Street's recent problems, you'd think the lack of it would be a good thing when looking for responsible management of major public corporations, where so much is already at risk for personal investors. Another recent study led by Clara Kulich of the University of Exeter in Britain found that men who turn around failing companies receive increased rewards in their bonuses of more than 260 percent, while women who do the same can expect a jump of 4 percent. The conclusion is that if women are being rewarded less for risk-taking, why should they take risks in the first place? Kulich's study also concludes that companies have lower expectations of women, see them as less credible, and not as influential of leaders as their male counterparts. "Low expectations of women can be as destructive as overt discrimination," wrote Susan Hockfield, a neuroscientist and president of Massachusetts Institute of Technology, in an essay published a few years ago by the *Boston Globe*. The first step to ending stereotypes is to publicly acknowledge them. Explanations of low expectations, a glass ceiling, a lack of testosterone, or a lack of ambition simply don't pass the smell test when it comes to explaining the gross inequities that exist for women in the corporate world.

There are some success stories that we as women should recognize and celebrate: Meg Whitman, recently retired from eBay's top position; Indra Nooyi, the chairman and chief executive of PepsiCo; Anne Mulcahy, the chairman and chief executive of Xerox; Lynn Laverty Elsenhans, chief executive at Sunoco; Angela Braly, the president and chief executive of WellPoint; Patricia Woertz, the chairman, president, and chief executive of Archer Daniels Midland Company; and Paula Rosput Reynolds, the chairman, president, and chief executive of Safeco Corp. Despite these successes, leaders acknowledge that women have a long way to go. "Corporate America needs to do a better job of proactively preventing discrimination and addressing complaints promptly and effectively," said Equal Employment Opportunity Commission Chair Naomi C. Earp last year. "To ensure that equality of opportunity becomes a reality in the twenty-first century workplace, employers need to place a premium on fostering inclusive and discrimination-free work environments for all individuals."

WORKPLACE

- Women make up 46 percent of the national workforce or 60 percent of all women nationally.
- According to the Bureau of Labor Statistics, in 2007, women were paid on average 76.5 percent of what their male counterparts were.
- The United States has the largest gender earnings gap of developed countries after Austria and Switzerland.
- According to the Equal Employment Opportunity Commission (EEOC), during 2007, workplace pregnancy discrimination charges surged to a record high level, up 14 percent from 2006.

- At the same time, sexual harassment filings were up 7 percent in 2007 to the highest level since 2002.
- According to the EEOC's 2007 data, allegations of discrimination in all major categories showed double digit percentage increases from the prior year—a rare occurrence.
- Of all the women who had children in 2006, nearly 60 percent worked.
- The median annual earnings of a female high school graduate were 34 percent less than those of her male counterpart.
- One year out of college, women working full-time earn 80 percent of what men earn, according to a study by the American Association of University Women Educational Foundation.

Forget about the argument of working moms versus stay-at-home moms; for a majority of women nowadays, working is not a choice but a necessity. Of those women I know who have to work to make ends meet, most are struggling to find jobs that pay them enough to cover their child care expenses and leave enough take-home money to make working worthwhile. Of those I know who choose to work who have children, almost all are in pursuit of what I call the "perfect part-time job," or a job that satisfies their professional and personal aspirations, without compromising their need to be great moms. In either case, the tough choices women are forced to make when it comes to working and family would be a whole lot easier if there didn't exist such a blatant pay discrepancy between men and women in the workplace.

Not only do women still only earn 76 percent of what men earn, but even in occupations dominated by women like education and nursing, disparities in pay still exist. For example, according to a report published in October of 2008 by the U.S. Department of Labor, Bureau of Labor Statistics, female elementary and middle school teachers earned nearly 10 percent less than similarly employed men, despite comprising 82 percent of the field. Female registered nurses earned more than 10 percent less than their male colleagues, although 90 percent of nurses are women, and female physicians and surgeons earned a whopping 41 percent less than their male counterparts.

But pay disparity is not the only problem right now; discrimination based on pregnancy is up to record-high levels, along with sexual harassment, which is reporting its sharpest increase since 2002. According to statistics by the Equal Employment Opportunity Commission, its call center logged more than 20,000 pregnancy discrimination complaints in 2007. Furthermore, the EEOC acknowledges that for every person who calls, there are thousands who have been discriminated against who do not seek any action. Let's make it clear right now: Discriminating on the basis of pregnancy is not only immoral, it's against the law and entitles you to damages. The Pregnancy Discrimination Act is an amendment (October 1978), to the Civil Rights Act of 1964 (www.eeoc.gov/policy/vii.html), which prohibits discrimination on the basis of pregnancy, childbirth, or related medical conditions. It not only protects you from on-the-job discrimination, it makes it illegal for an employer to refuse to hire you because you're pregnant. If you feel you've been unfairly discriminated against because of pregnancy, gender, or race, or been sexually harassed on the job, call the EEOC at 1-800-669-4000, to see what your rights are under the law, and whether you're entitled to damages by filing a complaint.

In addition, there's a new law in town to protect you from pay discrimination: On Jan. 28, 2009, President Obama signed into law the Lilly Ledbetter Fair Pay Act, expanding the statute of limitations for wage discrimination lawsuits to cover when an employee discerns a pay discrepancy. Lilly Ledbetter is a contemporary woman from Alabama who worked for Goodyear Tire and Rubber from 1979 to 1998. After early retirement from her job as an area manager, she discovered that she had been paid less than 15 men with the same title of area manager during her time with the company. After discovering that her claim exceeded the statue of limitations of 180 days for filing from the beginning of the alleged pay discrepancy, she took her case all the way to the Supreme Court and won by a 5 to 4 decision. Despite her victory in court, Ledbetter will never recover the disputed income owed her by Goodyear; she won on principle alone, selflessly fighting to make sure that other women would not be required to file pay discrimination claims within an impossibly narrow window of 180 days.

ACADEMIC

According to research by the American Association of University Professors (AAUP) and the U.S. Department of Labor, Bureau of Labor Statistics:

- Female college and university teachers earned more than 25 percent less than their male counterparts on average.

- Though women now receive about 6 in 10 college degrees, the AAUP's 2006 study on faculty gender equity reported that women held only 31 percent of tenured faculty positions.

- The median annual earnings of a woman with a bachelor's degree was almost 31 percent (or $15,911) less than that of a similarly qualified man.

- Women are more likely to complete graduate education. A woman with a master's degree earned 32 percent (or $21,374) less than a man with a master's degree.

- The median annual earnings for a woman with a professional degree were $65,941 while men earned over $100,000.

- A woman with a doctoral degree earned 29 percent (or $22,824) less than a similarly qualified man.

- Women have been earning more bachelor's degrees than men since 1982, and they have been earning more master's degrees than men since 1981.

Tenured professors comprise the highest ranks of the academic profession, and, accordingly, receive the highest pay. According to a report in 2007 by the AAUP, when it comes to tenure, women have nearly reached parity at community colleges, comprising 47 percent of tenured full-time faculty at these institutions, but that decreases to a little more than one-third at master's and baccalaureate degree-granting colleges, and only one-fourth at doctoral degree-granting universities where the pay is the highest. In addition to assigning top pay and recognition, tenure is important because it essentially guarantees professors lifetime employment, which is critical when you're taking risks in research, scholarly writing, or even the subject matter you teach. "Basically, the more prestigious the institution, the fewer the women there are," says the study's co-author Martha S. West, professor of law at University of California-Davis.

Again, the whole problem seems to come down to women making choices between career and family. The authors of the study stressed the importance of academia to convey to women that they no longer have to make a choice between raising children and becoming tenure-track faculty members. "We need to do a better job of publicizing the whole cultural shift [of the work-family ethic] and graduate students have to be convinced first," says West. And study co-author Dr. Ann Higginbotham suggests that though overt sexism might not be present on campuses, other subtle pressures related to work and family are. "Even though there's a lot of progress, we're not sure what's going on in terms of model programs [for work-family]," says Higginbotham. I don't know about you, but I think hiring equal numbers of women in tenure-track positions at equal pay would go a long way in convincing women that they don't have to make a choice between an academic career and family.

The report concludes that unless institutions establish a centralized review of all salaries at the time of appointment, salary inequities will continue far into the future. "As long as women hold 57 percent of the lecturer and instructor positions, but only 36 percent of the assistant through full professor positions, these significant differences between men's and women's average salaries will remain."

HOLLYWOOD

According to Martha M. Lauzen, Ph.D., the executive director of the Center for the Study of Women in Television & Film and the publisher of the annual report, The Celluloid Ceiling: Behind the Scenes Employment of Women:

- Women comprised 16 percent of all directors, executive producers, producers, writers, cinematographers, and editors working on the top 250 films during 2008, a decline of 3 percent from 2001 and an increase of 1 percent from 2007.
- Women accounted for 9 percent of directors in 2008, an increase of 3 percent from 2007. This figure represents no change from the percentage of women directing in 1998.
- Twenty-two percent of the films released in 2008 employed no women directors, executive producers, producers, writers, cinematographers, or editors. No films failed to employ a man in at least one of these roles.
- A historical comparison of women's employment on the top 250 films in 2008 and 1998 reveals that the percentages of women directors and cinematographers have remained stable, whereas the percentages of women writers, executive producers, producers, and editors have declined slightly.

Hollywood is more than just entertainment; it's a $10 billion a year business. Even in these economic times,

Hollywood has proven to be a bright spot, reporting a record haul of $9.78 billion in 2008, a 2 percent increase over 2007. Having equal opportunities to work in a recession-proof industry is important if women are to maintain gender equity in an economy where they are taking the brunt of the layoffs in other key sectors.

But Hollywood is more than just the business of entertainment; it's a cultural arbiter for not only the United States but the world, and the fact that women are underrepresented in the films that Hollywood produces seems to suggest that women's lives just aren't as important as men's. That's not my opinion, that's the opinion of legendary multiple Academy Award winning actress Meryl Streep. In an interview with ABC reporter Cynthia McFadden in February 2009, Streep lamented this fact: "We're still not telling everybody's story in our country and that's where we are." "Three of the nominated films this year have 26 men and 1 woman [in featured roles]. You know, we accept it. It's not unusual. But we would go nuts if three of the nominated films had 26 women and 1 man. It would be a very, very unusual thing." According to statistics posted on WomenAndHollywood.com, in 2008, only 6 of the top 50 grossing films (12 of the top 100 films) starred or were focused on women (based on *Variety's* list of top 250 grossing films). On top of that, studies by San Diego State University show that in 2008, women made up only 23 percent of film critics at the top 100 daily newspapers.

"Look around the world," Streep said, "women are living as we were in this country in the nineteenth century in many, many, many parts of the world. They're bartered, they are property, they don't have the rights we have—it's very difficult for us to understand all those things. But we do have a sense that for us, that's in the past." Still, Streep sees hope for women in Hollywood. "I think there's more opportunity now for actresses," she said, "interesting work [that's more] complicated and demanding stuff than there maybe was 20 years ago. Women in power are still kind of terrifying to us ... it's a complicated negotiation on the part of the person who has the authority and the people she's bossing around." Acknowledging the successes this year of Secretary of State Hillary Clinton and former Alaskan Governor and vice presidential candidate Sarah Palin, Streep said that we're not close to gender parity in Hollywood, but "we're on our way."

FAMILY

Things were already bad for women and children on domestic issues, but now economic pressures are hitting women and children harder than any segment in society.

- Women are 40 percent more likely than men to be living in poverty, with elderly women in the United States 60 percent more likely to be living in poverty.
- According to the Catholic Campaign for Human Development, children represent 36 percent of all impoverished people in the United States.
- In single-parent households headed by a female, more than half of the children are living in poverty, five times the rate of married-couple families.

- There are 3.5 million homeless people in the United States, or 1 percent of the population, and 39 percent of them (1.3 million) are children, according to a study by the National Law Center on Homelessness and Poverty.

According to research by the National Law Center on Homelessness & Poverty (www.nlchp.org), and a survey of the Association of Gospel Rescue Missions (AGRM), reported by *The Christian Post* in November of 2008 in a story by Eric Young titled "Survey: Homelessness Hitting Women, Children Hardest," women and children are experiencing an exponential rise in homelessness. Not only are women and children, particularly single mothers, more vulnerable to variables like higher food and fuel prices, now it's recession-induced layoffs and bank fore-closures on rental properties—a traditional housing option for lower-income individuals—that is pushing women and their children onto the streets and into shelters looking for assistance in record numbers. "We've got 325 beds available, and our mission is always full," reported John Anderson, president and CEO of the Bay Area Rescue Mission in Richmond, California. "In September 2008, we turned away more than 1,100 individuals, mostly women with children. We just didn't have room for them. Our turnaways have jumped more than 400 percent from the same month last year. The increase began in mid-July and has been steadily growing ever since." According to the AGRM survey, women with children made up 66 percent of the homeless, a jump from 55 percent in 2007 and the highest figure recorded by the national association in the last 8 years. This percentage is in comparison to 15 percent couples, 14 percent intact families, and 5 percent single men with children.

MIND-BLOWING

This startling rise in homelessness of women and children beginning in the middle of 2007 is a new phenomenon that is only just beginning to be documented. Who knows where it's going to lead? At the time that I'm writing this book, we're on the front end of this national foreclosure crisis driven by a historic reshaping of the United States' economy, creating a host of new challenges for women and children to deal with. What's clear by virtue of all these statistics is that women and their children were already at a significant disadvantage when it came to economic opportunities across the board on every level in our society. From all early indications, from the highest echelons of Wall Street to the lowest ranks of homelessness, this is not an equal-opportunity recession: Women are carrying a disproportionate burden of these economic hard times. Although the global downturn began in the world's financial sectors with wildly risky behavior in the unregulated mortgage markets, which are indisputably dominated by men and where even the experts agree that testosterone played a part, it is now bearing down on women and their children, most often found in low-wage and part-time jobs not only in the United States but around the world. At the same time the recession is rippling across the globe from wealthy to developing countries, where women lack safety nets to help them survive, putting the well-being of women and children across the world in jeopardy.

Fortunately, we're becoming uniquely empowered at the same time.

CHAPTER 3

Don't Get Angry, Get Rich

I asked you to hold your anger to the end. By now, you're probably pretty angry. Just when you thought it was safe to get angry, I'm going to tell you to *not* get angry, *get rich!*

SUCCESS IS THE BEST REVENGE

That's right. Don't waste a minute of your valuable time getting angry. Get busy getting rich instead! There's no profit in anger. Anger is just another sad trap. Anger is a dead end to failure. Anger is a waste of your precious time here on earth. Anger is what small people use to distract themselves from success. Sure, to everything there is a season and a time for every purpose under heaven. But your anger season better be short. Your anger better pick you up, dust you off, and send you on your way to success. Your anger better be the engine that moves you toward a bright and shiny future. Your anger better be a force of nature you harness to create good in the world instead of bad. Your anger better not ever be directed toward other women.

THIS ISN'T PERSONAL, IT'S BUSINESS

Nobody loves an angry person. Nobody wants to follow an angry leader. No good has ever come in this world from angry leaders. This world doesn't need any more angry people right now. There are so many people making money selling anger and fear right now, this world does not need any more. There is so much anger directed at powerful women from radio pundits, TV pundits, from women themselves—we need to stop it. This isn't personal, it's business.

In my own entrepreneurial journey from a stay-at-home mom with two little boys, a laid-off husband, and a two-hundred-thousand-dollar mortgage, I've had plenty of opportunities to be angry. Along the way I've learned a couple of very important lessons about anger, which I'm going to share with you. I could spend a lot of time recounting my experiences in some of the highest ranks of business, entertainment, and government from New York, to Los Angeles, and various points in between, in boardrooms and showrooms, in hotel rooms, and even bathrooms that brought me to this understanding, but I'm going to save that for another book and another time. For now, I'm going to sum up in a nutshell for you what I learned about anger.

Anger comes from having to ask; we're not asking anymore.

Anger comes from being powerless; we're not power-less anymore.

Anger comes from frustration working in a system that doesn't work for us; we're not working in the system any-more.

THE "F" WORD: FEMINIST

This word is so maligned, I don't want to use it anymore. This word has become a weapon for those who are mak-ing money selling anger and hate. Some of these people have saddled this word with so much derogatory conno-tation that it's become a word women are afraid to use, for fear of associating themselves with all the negative meaning attached to it. Many people have used this word to try to cast aspersions of a personal nature on women who have exercised their rights in the political process to achieve gender equity in order to support their families. They've tried to turn this from a political discussion to a personal one. But this isn't even a political discussion any-more; it's an economic discussion. We're not working in the political system anymore; we're commanding power through our control of this economy to take our fair share. Anybody who attacks women for wanting to succeed eco-nomically for their benefit and the benefit of their families is an angermonger, it's that simple. In women's revolution 2.0, don't call us feminists, call us boss.

COMMERCIALIZE YOUR ANGER

If you're going to be angry, find a way to commercialize it. That doesn't mean get on the radio and TV and get people all worked up with anger so you can make a couple of million dollars a year, all the while hating yourself for doing it. That market is pretty much glutted right now and the barriers to entry are high. Besides, women aren't allowed to be angry publicly. Commercializing your anger means finding a way to turn that energy into something you can use to inspire you to prove them all wrong, to make them wish they never said that, to show them what you're made of, to make them regret ever passing you up for that job. Find a way to turn the anger that stuns you, breaks your heart, and kicks you in the stomach, into something instead that causes you to stand up and fight for yourself, makes you fearless, tough, smart, and savvy—in short, makes you a force to be reckoned with.

THERE IS NO COURAGE WITHOUT VULNERABILITY

Just don't let a fear of making someone mad stop you from being passionate, taking risks, and standing up for yourself. I know as women we're all about trying to make everybody happy all the time. A lot of the survival skills we've learned in order to make it in this world are about going along to get along, trying to fit in, downplaying the fact that we're women while accepting what we're given. If you're going to get ahead in this new world you're going to have to be willing to break the rules. What people think about you as you're out there working outside of the status quo shouldn't be a factor in what you decide to do daily to get your share of success. The rules as they stand were meant to be broken. If you play by the rules as they are currently written, you're not going to get anywhere, as the facts plainly demonstrate. I'm going to be honest with you right up front: You're going to make a lot of people nervous by breaking the rules. Some of them are undoubtedly going to be your family and friends. Some of them are going to try and get you to stop, to conform, to fit back into the system. You're just going to have to learn to tune them out.

FOLLOW THE MONEY

But don't fight any battles where money isn't the end game. When it comes to deciding what battles are worth fighting and what battles aren't, use this simple rule: Follow the money. When it comes to letting what other people think of you influence your thoughts or actions, ask yourself," "Where's the money?" If doing things outside of the system, making people nervous and attracting criticism brings you closer to taking control of your financial destiny, that's where you should be. If it's not bringing you one step closer to money on a daily basis, then you're on the wrong path.

YOU CAN ALWAYS TELL A LEADER BY THE ARROWS IN HER BACK

Just don't internalize the criticism. The same goes for anger. That means don't deal with emotions that come from conflict by only thinking about them rather than expressing them openly. If you come up against an insurmountable wall and take a stand for yourself, making people nervous, maybe even angry, and you fail, don't blame yourself. Don't beat yourself up. Don't apologize for your passion. Don't apologize for sticking up for yourself.

Don't ever apologize for challenging injustice whenever and wherever you see it. Instead, give yourself credit for having the courage to knock on a door, to try and push it open, to express your dissatisfaction or your expectation for fairness. Don't let anybody tell you to be quiet. It takes guts to walk a different path from what is expected of you as a woman or a mom, but what's your choice? You'll soon discover that each step you take brings you new freedom and happiness and power and passion that you never knew you had. But people are jealous of power and passion, even if it's just power over your own life and passion for what you're doing. Some of them, either consciously or unconsciously, are going to try to sabotage your success by trying to make you feel guilty or wrong. That's just a fact. Don't try and fix it. Just tune it out and keep going. Eventually, you'll see, they'll come around to seeing things the way you do. It happens every time, although it takes longer for some people to do so than others.

DON'T LET ANYBODY TELL YOU TO BE QUIET

People tell me to be quiet all the time. People told me not to write this book. This book is a testimony to the commercialization of anger. This book is a refusal to internalize criticism. This book is a slap in the face of the status quo. Friends of mine who read this book in its initial stages told me that I was going to have to become a lesbian, because there wouldn't be a man on earth who wasn't going to be intimidated by me. I don't think so. The intimidation part, I mean. I love men: metrosexual London men, Latin men, linebacker men, bookish intellectuals, backwoods men, city-of-the-broad-shoulders Chicago men, and my favorite, men who love their children. Nobody's a bigger fan of men than me. Real men aren't intimidated by real women like us. Any man who hates women like us is obviously trying to overcompensate for other deficiencies.

I LOVE MEN

This is not an anti-man campaign. This isn't a women's revolution, this is a family revolution. I want to empower men to take control of their financial destiny as much as I want to empower women. It's women and children first, that's all. Men are struggling in this system, too, particularly men of color and gay men, as well as men who have been downsized, men whose skills are becoming obsolete, men who are getting older, and men who carry the full burden of having to provide for their families in an increasingly-competitive economic climate. Decent men who are just trying to make an honest living and want no part of limiting women's opportunities in the workplace or the world want to see change as much as we do. In the New Economy, everything is changing, including gender roles as they relate to both work and family. Everything is being recreated, redefined, all the rules are being broken, and new ones are being made, which is just as liberating for men who have been forced to sacrifice their family time for jobs they often hate, as it is for women.

"Anything's possible if you've got enough nerve."
—J.K. Rowling

THE SECRET TO MY SUCCESS

Can you believe the secret of my success boils down to one simple factor? It's nerve, or as my friends from New York like to call it, *chutzpah*. Chutzpah, or nerve, is a mixture of boldness and confidence you use to get what you want in this world. It's amazing how powerful it is. It's so simple yet effective, it's almost like magic. I didn't know it was that simple myself until the most successful person I know, my dear mentor, an "old boy" master of the universe who has had a hand in creating some of the world's biggest, most profitable companies, told me that that quality alone was what I had to thank for getting me where I am today. I'll tell you more about what it is and how to get it later in this book. For now, let's just call it an ability to create the life you really want by acting with courage, conviction, and a refusal to take "no" for an answer. That doesn't mean you act recklessly. It doesn't mean you're not afraid. It never means acting rudely. It doesn't mean you don't have fear and doubts. It just means you look fear and doubt squarely in the face every morning and consciously push them aside and tell them to get out of your way. It doesn't mean you don't feel the slings and arrows that inevitably storm upon a leader, sometimes making you cry at the end of the day. It just means taking the arrows in your back as you push ahead, pausing a moment to take them out and care for yourself, then summoning new courage to keep moving forward. Pretty soon you're simply not content to stand still anymore, to be quiet, to accept the status quo. It doesn't take long before you discover the power that acting with nerve and confidence brings to making your fondest dreams and wishes come true. Then you become addicted to the adrenaline that comes from taking risks, pushing yourself to new boundaries, and achieving successes you never thought possible.

WHO DO YOU THINK YOU ARE?

Now that I've got your attention, I'll tell you who you are. You're it! You're hot, beautiful, and smart; you deserve success and it's yours for the taking! People tell me, "I could never be like you." Oh yes you can! I've learned that being a flawed human being is actually an asset when it comes to becoming successful at whatever you do, including becoming a millionaire. I don't accept it when people tell me they could never be as confident as I am or do the things that I've done. Not true! I'm just like many of you, the product of an underprivileged, dysfunctional family upbringing that screwed up my self-esteem until I found a way to fix it on my own by walking through the fire of doubt and anxiety. I beat fear by confronting it head on, pushing myself to do things that were terrifying, mortifying, physically and emotionally challenging, while becoming stronger with each new trial. All the successful people I've met along the way were pretty much the same as me: real human beings with something to prove, some need to redeem themselves, or some unstoppable drive to fix something in themselves that was broken. So don't tell me you can't do this. Just believe in yourself and go after what you want. Convert the anger to passion, push aside doubt and fear, pull out the arrows that are going to follow you, take care of yourself first, then take what's yours. Don't be afraid of rocking the boat and don't spend one minute trying to make everybody happy. I'll tell you what I told my kids' school principal: I'm not here to make friends; I'm here to advocate for my children. In the business world, you're not here to make friends, either. You're here to make money. If you can let go of the urge to make everybody happy and be everybody's friend all the time, you're going to be successful.

ONLY THE GOOD SUCCEED

On the other hand, don't think that courtesy and professionalism aren't important. In my experience, the higher I've gone up in the world, the more I've seen evidence that only the good succeed. The first rule of success is that integrity is the most precious thing you possess and you must protect it at all costs. It's the roadmap by which you guide yourself through the minefield of personal and professional relationships that make up business and life. Compromise your integrity just once, and you've lost it forever. That's how precious integrity is. Business, like life, is all about relationships, and once people have lost faith that you will act honestly and fairly in a business transaction, you can rarely earn that faith and trust back. Call it karma, or the Golden Rule, it's never been more true that you get back what you put out, and that treating people as you would want to be treated yourself yields bountiful, almost magical returns.

Believe me, the people I've met who could afford to be the rudest to me because of their preeminent standing in the professional world, whether it was publishing, entertainment, retail, or even private equity, have always been the kindest, most polite, most considerate, helpful, respectful people I meet. You would think the opposite would be true, and a lot of people must assume so because I frequently meet people on their way up who confuse superiority with success. Believe me, when you come into a meeting or a business relationship with that attitude, everybody's talking about it and you when you leave the room. Class is another thing that people seem to be confused about. The measure of class is not how well you dress, or how attractive you look, or what college you graduated from, or what your family background is; class is measured in how you treat others. The people who were the most accomplished and successful people I met at the top would show the same courtesy and respect to every person they met throughout their day, regardless of what they looked like, how they dressed, or what job they needed to do to support themselves and their familes.

THE IMPORTANCE OF ATTITUDE

I was shocked on one of my recent trips to Los Angeles to learn that all you needed to possess in order to get a dream job in one of the most competitive cites on earth was the right attitude. I was also equally shocked to learn that the right attitude was in painful short supply in this extremely competitive city. On this particular trip I was chauffeured around by a brand new production assistant working for one of Hollywood's best production companies. I couldn't believe, and it seemed that he couldn't either, that he came to Hollywood without a film degree from UCLA or any of the other great film schools, in fact, just an English degree from an ordinary public university in the south, and got a job that thousands of people with film degrees from the best schools were standing in line behind him for. When I asked his boss why he picked him, he said it was because out of all the hundreds of people they could have chosen, he was the only one who enthusiastically wanted the job—and any chore that went along with it, including driving me around town all day through L.A. traffic—without feeling entitled to it.

> "The question isn't who is going to let me; it's who is going to stop me."
>
> —Ayn Rand

IT'S NOT POLITICAL, IT'S PERSONAL

So you see the time for being angry is over. The time for getting rich is here, and it begins with attitude. We not only have to redefine the behaviors that are expected of women in the workplace and in the business world, we have to redefine our attitudes toward ourselves and our success. In my experience, women undervalue themselves in every endeavor across the board. Even I have to remind myself regularly of the value of my work and its cost to others. On top of that, women are unfortunately often expected to work for free or at a discount, particularly on projects that cater to women, like charities. It's time for us to have higher expectations for ourselves, our ambitions, our pay, and our businesses. We can't count on the opinions of our peers, friends, or families any more to give us the recognition and reinforcement that is critical to developing the self-worth necessary to take our share, because it's not there! We're not getting those messages from the media, the workplace, our educational institutions, and sadly, often not from our friends or family. We have to create and develop our own inner resources that provide us with daily affirmations of how beautiful, powerful, and deserving of success we are. This book is a beginning.

OLDER WOMEN VERSUS YOUNGER WOMEN

I've seen enough to know that there's a difference in the way older and younger women are responding to these social and economic realities we're facing. It blew my mind this year to work with a couple of women in their fifties, who were intimately connected to one of the highest offices of government, and who were leaders in their communities on important charities, universities, and boards while enjoying some of the highest levels of social standing and respect in the state—who were immeasurably angrier and more militant than me. I later found out that these were the same women who had to risk life and limb to provide medical services to poor women at Planned Parenthood during the years when protesters were throwing bombs over the fence. They were the women who went into the heart of the urban ghettos to provide lifelines of resources and money to women and their children who were living with every kind of sadness and challenge imaginable. These women, though eminently accomplished and with every kind of privilege available to them, chose to stay in the system and work to help those women who could not get out of it. These women concealed a fire underneath their calm exterior that would make anything I have written so far on these pages look like a child's bedtime story. Keep that in mind the next time you go to a fancy black-tie social event where such women are ensconced in their element, and consider them from afar with respect and caution.

Then there are the young twenty-something professional women I meet who don't seem to have a clue that
any gender inequities exist in our society. I've found that
they either haven't yet had enough experience in the workplace to have had any firsthand encounters with discrimination or that they've already made the choice to drop out
of the system altogether and start their own businesses. I'm
encouraged to see that for them, this discussion appears
to be moot; they're already empowered enough to see the
opportunity that exists for them to take control of their
financial destiny, and they go after it. But these women
are decidedly in the minority.

THE PENALTY IS CHILDREN

It doesn't appear that the big wake-up call comes for
women until children enter the picture. Everything inside
and outside of the system is manageable, until you throw in
this monkey wrench. Studies in the late 1990s in the United
States and Britain confirmed that having children nega-
tively impacts the pay of women in the workplace. One
study published in the journal of the University of Chicago
attributed 40 to 50 percent of the gender wage gap to
having kids.* Another study determined that U.S. women
experience a 7 percent wage penalty per child, attributing
the reduction in pay to factors such as skill loss, reduced
work hours, or outright discrimination (www.asanet.org/
galleries/default-file/motherwage.pdf).

But it's not just women that are making the tough
choice between career and family, men are feeling the
stress, too. According to a report by the American

*www.journals.uchicago.edu/doi/abs/10.1086/209897.

Association of University Women, survey results found that a majority of both men (74 percent) and women (83 percent) would choose a job that had lower pay but provided benefits such as family leave, flexible hours, and help with family care. What's sadly ironic is that this same study found that among college-educated adults, the men (55 percent) were more likely to have flextime options at their workplace for caring for family members than were women (39.7 percent), who are the primary caregivers for most children in this country. It is apparent that making the workplace a more family-friendly environment through flextime and job sharing would not only be a welcome option for both women and men, it would no doubt make our kids happier, too.

TUNE IN, DROP OUT

In my experience, the "children penalty" is not only the primary factor contributing to gender inequity issues in this country, it's what's driving the country's current entrepreneurial revolution, which is being led by women who are starting new businesses today at twice the rate of men. Fed up with the corporate world that penalizes them for being both women and mothers, women are taking their own destinies into their hands and following their dreams in record numbers. It's become apparent to me that most women I know are starting these businesses as a lifestyle choice, as a means to balance their personal and professional career aspirations with their need to be great moms, and research seems to prove that. Out of 38 million women with children in the United States, two-thirds of the working moms who responded to a recent poll by Oprah said they would quit work and stay home with their kids if they could. But staying at home isn't the answer for a lot of women anymore. The same poll conducted by Oprah showed that among the stay-at-home moms, more than one-third wished they worked outside the home.

BUT YOU CAN HAVE IT ALL

The truth is, the technology of the twenty-first century is changing our daily lives in new and revolutionary ways, radically transforming the 9 to 5 workday and family world. Forget about that old argument that "women can have it all, just not at the same time." That's not true anymore: You can have it all and I'm proof. If you read my first book, *Mommy Millionaire*, you know that I resolved very early in my entrepreneurial journey that if I was going to endure all the risk and hard work that was involved in starting my own business, and I couldn't take my kids with me, I wasn't going. I'm living proof that there's a new way of living available to women, and the time to choose it is now.

HOW DO YOU LIKE US NOW?

Not only are there more than 11 million women entrepreneurs in this country, representing 48 percent of all businesses, but the U.S. Census Bureau predicts that by 2015 that number will climb to 55 percent. Yeah baby, that's a majority. With 70 percent of all jobs in the United States created by small businesses, women, fueled by nothing less than an uncompromising, unstoppable love for their children, are what very well could prove to rescue this country from its current testosterone-driven financial meltdown, which will no doubt be recorded in history as one of the most obscene and immoral abuses of greed and power any modern-day civilization has seen.

Is there a figure any more detested by our popular culture than the lowly mommy? Could we be seen as any more weak or powerless? Is it possible that the most marginalized demographic in U.S. society, namely moms, is suddenly the most powerful group on earth? You bet it is! It's time for us to rewrite this whole mom thing, but this time we're going to be smart, beautiful, powerful, and rich. (Oh, and all our kids will be gifted and well-behaved, too.) When we're done with this, mom will be the new sexy. We're going to be wiping butts and taking names by the time 2015 rolls around.

FIRST THE UNITED STATES, THEN THE WORLD

Wow, just when we really needed an entrepreneurial revolution, remaking the economy as we know it by driving innovation while simultaneously creating employment and investment opportunities for all, here we are, in the driver's seat, ready to take control, clean up somebody else's mess and deliver a bright future for ourselves and our families. Good thing we got all our anger issues under control here first.

SHOW ME THE MONEY

Thirty-eight million women with children control $8.5 trillion in consumer spending every year—three-quarters of the U.S. economy. At the same time, women-owned businesses employ approximately 27 million people and are responsible for more than $3.6 trillion in business-related purchases each year, with those numbers growing exponentially every year. Put this together with a revolutionary new ability to communicate with each other in real time, and you can see that we have leverage. I'm going to show you how to use it.

CHAPTER 4

The New Economy

RULES OF THE NEW ECONOMY

Forget about everything you heard about the death of the U.S. economy. It's not dying; it's being reborn! What we're going through right now economically is not the sickness, it's the cure. We were sick before; this is the antidote.

I'm not an economist. But I am an entrepreneur, and the one thing that is common to every entrepreneur is that we're realists—especially when it comes to money. At the end of the month, when we have to make payroll, we might be forced to take emergency second mortgages out on our houses, because nobody from the government is going to sweep in at the last minute to deliver *us* a bundle of cash. As an entrepreneur living in the real world, I know that times like these are a necessary evil, a correction that is going to hurt, but afterward the fever will break and we'll have sweated out all that nasty stuff that is making us sick, like inflated home prices, trade deficits, and exponential debt. The bubble that was powered by irresponsible lending practices by financial institutions over the last 10 years, not just in the United States but around the world, has burst. Now it's time to push restart and reboot the economy, which is resulting in a historic leveling of the playing field between big business and small business, creating incredible opportunity for those creative and visionary enough to see it . . . and courageous enough to go for it.

DON'T PANIC—REACT!

I don't spend one minute anymore listening to predictions from the so-called experts about what's going to happen in this economy. The fact is, nobody really knows what's going to happen. Those same experts at all the most so-phisticated financial reporting sources who are wringing their hands and saying this is the end of U.S. capitalism as we know it, didn't even see this economic tsunami coming, until it was too late. Part of the problem is that financial markets and even global economies are driven by human factors like fear and confidence—and nobody's got that information market cornered.

When it comes to predicting what's going to happen in the near or long-term future, don't listen to anybody because nobody knows for sure what's going to happen next, or where tomorrow's opportunities lie. Tomorrow's opportunities are being created today, by people you never heard of, who are no doubt working at their kitchen tables or in their garages, on money-making ideas that only maybe a handful of people in the world are visionary enough to see. Ignore the cynics and focus instead like a laser beam on your business or your dream and start working like crazy to make it a reality. This country has always been and will always be about betting on crazy hopes and dreams, making people rich, and giving people jobs as a result. That is not going to change any time soon.

One thing's for sure, some of the smartest and richest people in the world wait their whole lives for times like these to get richer. "Be fearful when others are greedy, and be greedy when others are fearful," goes Warren Buffett's cardinal rule of investing, which means act with courage and take risks when everyone else is acting with fear. Don't be one of those people who lets fear control your life. Believe it or not I think fear can be a good thing; it's the motivator that has probably driven as much action, innovation, and success as greed or any of the nobler passions like justice or love. The worst thing you can do is be afraid and do nothing. The antidote to fear is action.

> Becoming a millionaire means learning to recognize that fear can be conquered through information, where others allow a lack of information to create fear.
> —from *Mommy Millionaire*

Another priceless piece of advice for times like these comes from legendary stock market timer Don Wolanchuk, who says that historically, "the size of the advance is equal to the proportion of the decline." Translated, this means get busy, getting ready to get rich! All we need is a fresh wind of consumer confidence to blow away all the fear that clouds our current vision of the economic future, and things could change overnight. There are so many good things happening already: a low dollar that is making U.S. goods more affordable around the world; low energy costs that are driving consumer prices down dramatically; and market vulnerability on almost every industry front I can see that is lowering barriers to entry and making it easier for the new businesses to wrestle market share from the big guys through innovation, competition, and agility. At the same time, I see so many new technologies and social trends creating a dizzying array of products and new markets to take them directly to consumers that I believe we may be entering an epic period of historical significance equal to the Renaissance or the Industrial Revolution.

I'M DONE WITH THE PESSIMISM

In fact, there's so much opportunity in this New Economy, my head is spinning. I get so excited seeing how things are changing around me in the business world nowadays, I have to sometimes calm myself down! My company's creative director comes up with a new million dollar idea at least every other week. Even her 12-year-old son sees money-making opportunities around him that the most creative people at the biggest corporations don't, earning him invitations to meet with corporate product research and development people and television producers alike. In fact, the kid's already got his own patents! My own son started his own business this year at age 12, building and selling skateboard ramps, along the way designing his own logo and creating a social networking community around his brand. That's American entrepreneurialism! It's a genie in a bottle that's being let out by an economy transforming under economic and global pressures that come around once every hundred years.

GET YOUR SHARE!

Regardless of how you feel about change, you're going to have to accept it as part of the New Economy. What is the New Economy? It's different from everything else that's come before. The biggest mistake you can make right now is to think that things are going to return to "normal," or in this case, that you're going to wait out this recession successfully on unemployment benefits alone. We were in the midst of one of the greatest entrepreneurial surges in U.S. history before the recent economic shift made everybody an entrepreneur. There were more new businesses started in 2007 in the United States than at the height of the dot.com hysteria of the late 1990s, and this country is still the best place in the world to start them. The new law of survival demands that you take your financial destiny into your own hands. Educating ourselves as consumers and businesspeople as to the reality of the current economic climate is the first step to intelligently taking control of our destiny in it. That's why I put together these rules.

RULE #1: EVERYTHING IS CHANGING—DON'T CONFUSE CHANGE WITH FEAR

The facts cannot be ignored: Recent government statistics show that over five million jobs have been lost in the last year alone, racking up a national unemployment rate at its highest level in 25 years. A lot of those jobs are not coming back, at least not anytime soon. Whether or not you're an entrepreneur by choice, you're going to have to learn to think like one now. The sooner you accept this as a reality, the more successful you're going to be in adapting to the New Economy. Fortunately, women are already thinking like this, starting businesses at two times the rate of men. We already were working outside of the system, so let's take this momentum and show them who's boss.

On top of historic unemployment levels, the financial industry as we know it is being totally remade. If you're going to be forced to take control of your financial destiny by starting your own business, you're going to be forced to learn to bootstrap your business on the cheap in ever more creative ways, or find money to start or grow your business from nontraditional sources, such as private equity. The good news is that it's never been easier to do these things, particularly if you're a woman. As the top early adopters of new technology, women, particularly moms, are mastering the new tools of technology, communication, and social media at rates higher even than young men and using those skills to create, market, and sell their products in radical new ways, as I'll show you later in this book.

With unprecedented change comes unprecedented opportunity. As big businesses fail, small businesses will rise up to fill the void, capitalizing on market vulnerability through innovation, nimbleness, and invention. Forget about billion dollar companies, run your own company from your kitchen table with no expectation outside of supporting your family, and you'll discover a newfound freedom that comes from controlling your own financial destiny that you never thought was possible. With five million people looking for new economic opportunities in the greatest laboratory in the world for product innovation and free market capitalism, you know something great is bound to happen, like maybe the biggest entrepreneurial renaissance this country has ever seen.

See the change, be the change, take advantage of the opportunity, be creative and fearless, and survive.

RULE #2: PRIVATE EQUITY—THE NEW BANK

It takes money to make money and with traditional lending sources like banks dramatically cutting back on loans to businesses in response to the credit bubble bursting, entrepreneurs are turning to private equity as the bank of the future. At the same time, investment of private equity in new businesses is growing exponentially each year, bringing unprecedented capital resources within the reach of even modest business models. Private equity is money that comes from private investors who are licensed through the Securities and Exchange Commission (SEC). There are two forms of private equity capital typically available to start-up and mid-stage entrepreneurs: venture capital (VC) and angel capital.

Angel investors are certified by the SEC to be "high net worth individuals" with minimum liquid assets (cash) of $2,000,000 and minimum average salaries of $250,000 a year. They are private investors who usually come together in groups in their community for the purpose of stimulating economic growth and development, while reaping financial returns much higher than any other traditional investment vehicle typically available. Angels fund 30 to 40 times as many companies as venture capitalists every year, even though most people have never heard of them. Venture capital is private equity money usually reserved for second-stage companies in a high growth mode, or start-ups with an exceptionally strong business plan. A typical venture capital deal usually starts at a minimum $1,000,000 investment, while I've seen angels invest as little as $50,000 in a start-up. You can read all about my successful journey to raise angel capital in my first book *Mommy Millionaire*.

What's important for you to know now is that despite women owning 48 percent of all businesses, only 4 percent of angel capital goes to woman-owned businesses each year. As a response, the Kauffman Foundation, the nation's premiere entrepreneurial foundation, has issued a mandate to investors to invest in women-owned companies. In short, there's never been a better time to raise capital to start or grow your business!

The whole idea that you have to be Bill Gates or Steve Jobs, or be running a high-tech billion dollar venture to raise private equity money is false, as the following statistics from www.angelsoft.net show. Not only are the number of deals made through the fourth quarter of 2008 showing exponential growth, despite all the bad economic news and the meltdown of one segment of the traditional banking industry, but high-tech industries like biotechnology, semiconductors, computers, and networking come in almost last on the list of percentage of deals funded.

TOP 10 INDUSTRIES FUNDED BY ANGELS IN 2008

1. Consumer products and services—13.3 percent
2. Media and entertainment—12.9 percent
3. Software—12.7 percent
4. Business products and services—7.8 percent

5. IT Services—5.3 percent

6. Industrial/energy—4.8 percent

7. Medical devices and equipment—4.3 percent

8. Retailing/distribution—4.2 percent

9. Health care services—3.8 percent

10. Other—17.1 percent

Niche industries include biotechnology, 3.6 percent; financial services, 3.5 percent; telecommunications, 3.2 percent; electronics, 1.6 percent; computers and peripherals, 0.9 percent; networking and equipment, 0.5 percent; and semiconductors, 0.5 percent.

Even the private equity experts of Silicon Valley in one of their recent industry roundtable events concluded that although deals are being scrutinized more carefully than ever before, with a priority on revenues coming in the door at the business's inception, it's cheaper than ever to run a startup. And innovation, powered by capital, will continue to thrive in the New Economy.

BUT DON'T STOP THERE

Even the private equity community is being reinvented during this period of economic transformation. Some of my more visionary and daring acquaintances are predicting the end of the stock market as we know it, as private investors find new ways to connect their money with those entrepreneurs who are delivering an average of 30 percent returns on that investment. I've met many entrepreneurs myself who are finding new and original ways to connect with investors, too. One of them was a woman in Canada who owned a vineyard and winery and who also made a terrific line of skin care products on the side. To fund the growth of her business she sold small stakes in it for a few thousand dollars each. All the stakeholders were invited to an annual event where they picnicked and drank wine and celebrated the community and the land that they loved. They also each got weekend privileges for a guesthouse on the property, located in the midst of the vineyard with sweeping panoramic views. It was the experience and the community that the investors seemed to treasure more than the actual return on investment. Soon the woman had sold $150,000 worth of stakes with little effort, enabling her to buy more land and increase her wine production without a lot of the meddlesome oversight that comes with investors focused solely on the bottom line. That's just one story of many I've heard on my journey across the United States and Canada about small business owners on the front line who are finding creative solutions to the same problems people in the corporate world and the media spend a lot of time lamenting. With all the problems we've seen recently resulting from overleveraged, complex, and unregulated investment vehicles, maybe the answer for the future lies in the creation of small regional banks and private investors who actually can see, touch, and feel the businesses they're investing in. And maybe that answer—and opportunity—is being invented in massive, grassroots ways now.

RULE #3: ENTREPRENEURS ARE THE NEW ROCK STARS

When we think of rock stars we think of people who are rich, sexy, self-determined, creative, living the life of their dreams by a wing and a prayer. They are people who took a big gamble on a dream, trusted in their talent and won, resulting in adoring fans who either want to be like them or be with them. Sometimes they win, sometimes they lose, but we love them for trying. Music is a business, whether it's rock or rap or country or classical, and the most successful musicians are the people who have found a way to combine their passion and talents with good business sense. The same goes for entrepreneurs. There are a million people out there with good ideas; it's the people who take those ideas, fueled by passion, courage, and a willingness to take risks based on solid business principles that turn their ideas into millions—making us want to be like them or be with them. They are the new rock stars. When it comes to defining "crazy, sexy, cool" in today's cultural landscape, at the top of the list is entrepreneur. When even today's rap and rock stars aspire to become entrepreneurs, it's become even sexier to say you're in a start-up than to say you're in a band.

Entrepreneurs Are the New Heroes

Entrepreneurs are the people who are creating tomorrow's employment and investment opportunities today. They're almost always putting every dollar they own on the line, following some crazy dream while working long hours to create the jobs that most of the people in this country depend on. Unlike big corporations, they're operating without a safety net, and nobody swoops in with a bailout when they have to take out those second or third emergency mortgages on their homes to make payroll. These are the people who, instead of wringing their hands and waiting for someone to make a job happen for them, or waiting for a government bailout, are showing courage and character and guts at a time when many people are searching for courage and character and guts: in other words, searching for leadership.

The Entrepreneur Virus

I've heard that entrepreneurialism is a viral condition. The idea is that all you need to do is come in contact with someone whose mind has opened up to entrepreneurial opportunity to catch that virus—which I'll define here as the condition of seeing opportunity all around you. I know this is true in my life. Just knowing that my millionaire mentors took an idea from start up to a successful exit strategy in nine years seemed to give me insight, or maybe permission, to believe that I could do it, too. It was as if a door had opened in a room that I had become accustomed to living in my whole life—get a job, a career, buy the big house and SUV—to reveal a whole other part of a house that I had never seen before, with bigger rooms and lots more light. Suddenly I saw how becoming an entrepreneur and taking control of my financial destiny could bring the possibility of so much more freedom and satisfaction to my life.

If entrepreneurialism is a virus, then the cure has got to be in a business plan. Getting the virus comes from seeing opportunity in an idea. Curing the virus requires writing a business plan and forcing yourself to answer all the questions that go along with turning that great idea into a reality.

Entrepreneurs Are the New Leaders

Forget about politicians, the vision for this country is coming from the front lines of business. You can't legislate employment, even though it appears some political leaders think this is an option. You can't create a healthy and viable economy by pouring billions into companies that are failed business models to begin with. You just can't polish that turd, no matter how hard you try. That's not a political viewpoint, that's just economic reality. You can't spend billions retraining for jobs without creating the jobs first. With small business responsible for 70 percent of new job creation in this country, and women starting businesses at twice the rate of men, women are our de facto leaders. Any questions?

RULE #4: MOM IS THE NEW GREEN

It just makes sense that if we're starting all these businesses, taking on all this risk, leading our country with courage and resolve toward an economic future built on real-world viability that you *Buy Mom*™. Just as the green movement revolutionized almost every industry on earth, rebirthing opportunity by driving issues of sustainability and renewable resources into products, policy, and process, creating a whole new wave of innovation and companies in its wake, the *Buy Mom* movement is about to do the same. It's part of the plan that goes along with "don't get angry—get rich!"

The green movement has grown exponentially in the last three years, putting pressure on manufacturers, retailers, farmers, schools—everyone—to find alternative earth-friendly solutions to everything from toilet paper to power plants. According to Mintel Research, a leading global supplier of market intelligence, the number of Americans who say they almost always or regularly buy green products tripled in 2008 to 36 percent, up from 12 percent in 2007. Even despite current economic pressures that are expected to impact retail sales through 2013, causing consumers to choose products based on cost over green factor, predictions are for a 19 percent growth rate in the green products marketplace. The same research showed that 52 percent of shoppers who buy household cleaning supplies would buy green first if given a choice, provided they weren't too expensive. Even by conservative standards, the household cleaning supply market is worth over $7 billion dollars a year, making an earth-friendly alternative cleaning market worth more than $3.5 billion a year.

That's the known. Now take the unknown. The same powerful and transforming social forces that drove innovation and opportunity in the green market, namely environmental sustainability and consciousness, are about to remake every consumer market in the United States. But this time that innovation and opportunity will be driven by *economic* sustainability and consciousness instead of environmental. Once women figure out that the power they wield in the consumer marketplace, controlling $8.5 trillion in household spending and another $3.6 trillion in business spending, can be directed to supporting mom-made products—we'll experience a tidal wave of supply driven by that new demand. And why shouldn't we support each other by buying mom-made products? We're the leaders, taking the risks to create the jobs that are remaking the U.S. economy in historic and revolutionary ways, without any bailouts, or handouts, or corporate jets, or executive bonuses, stock options, or political action committee money or donors—you get the picture.

RULE #5: SMALL IS THE NEW BIG

That's why small is the new big. If moms are the new green, using their influence to create social pressures on markets to buy mom-made products instead of those that already exist in the marketplace, somebody is going to have to create all those new products to satisfy that demand. The reality is, even before the mom phenomenon hits there has been room for a million new products to be brought to the marketplace, and nobody knows what the consumer marketplace needs more than the ultimate consumer—moms. It doesn't take a genius to do the math on how big this opportunity is.

Add in market and social pressures like buy-local and buy-American, and you can see what kind of opportunity this creates for everyone—man or woman—from suppliers, to manufacturers, to marketers, to service providers like accountants and lawyers and web site developers. But don't take my word for it. Some expert trend-forecasters, employed by the biggest corporations in the United States to keep them ahead of the curve when it comes to buying trends, saw this coming years ago. One of these people is Marita Wesely-Clough, who *American Demographics* magazine identified as one of the top five trend spotters in the nation. She predicted an entrepreneurial age in which young companies produce new, ingenious products and devise new strategies to take their products direct to consumers. What, now we're going to let a little recession stop us? I don't think so! In fact, I see this recession as being the catalyst that's going to speed up these trends and market forces to create the innovation that this New Economy needs to keep itself from stagnating and dying in the clutches of economic and social models that have simply outlived their relevancy.

Anybody who tells you that the opportunities for employment or wealth are disappearing in this economy forever, never to return, are wrong. The only place jobs and investment dollars are decreasing is in the big corporations where there was probably too much redundancy or stagnation in the first place. What's going on now is a necessary purging that is going to open the doors and lower the barriers to entry to small business to pick up the slack. I could recount a hundred different instances of this in my own experience on the front lines of this new business economy in the last few years. One of them involved a friend of mine who owns a powder-coating business, where he coats metals for the automotive and office furniture industries. He told me that for the first time in five years he is able to compete on price with Chinese manufacturers, primarily because of the weakness of the dollar as a currency in the world, making it cheaper than ever for international manufacturers to buy American. Given the choice of buying American, with shorter production cycles, smaller orders, and competitive prices compared with Chinese offerings, the major corporations who subcontract these services always choose him. Another example occurred when one of the big three automakers in Michigan decided to outsource some of its metal-cutting functions rather than invest in new technology to do it in house. A friend of mine who owned a small shop that specialized in laser cutting of metal experienced a business boom that sent his revenues off the charts and into a rapid growth mode. Believe me, this is the United States; no business is too big to fail. If it does, a hundred small shops owned by a hundred small business owners, will pounce upon that opportunity to create thousands of new jobs to take the old one's place as fast as fire consumes oxygen. Nature abhors a vacuum, especially in business. Especially in the United States.

RULE #6: INNOVATE OR DIE

Which means get busy getting rich. I've already shown you all the opportunity that is being created by all this change. You're either part of the change, or you're part of the problem. People will always need consumer products, despite these current economic pressures. Consumer products are a recession-proof industry. No matter how much income you have or don't have, you're going to have to spend some of it on toilet paper, cleaning supplies, clothing, food, and an uncountable list of other products that make up the basic needs of daily living. That's why companies that specialize in simple consumer goods are not only surviving in these changing economic times, they're thriving. For instance, Kroger, the nation's largest grocery retailer, saw an increase in earnings of 8 percent in the first quarter of this year, with Wal-Mart reporting an increase of 2.8 percent in same-store sales during the same period. Same-store sales are considered the leading indicator of retail health.

With savvy consumers willing and able to make a choice, there's never been a better opportunity to bring innovative products to the marketplace around social issues. In fact, there's a name for it: social entrepreneurship. Social entrepreneurship has come to mean many different things to many different people, but a simple explanation for it here is the exploitation of any market around a social cause. From where I stand, the green movement

65

pioneered the social entrepreneurship movement. It created all kinds of product innovation and market opportunity while bringing attention to sustainability issues like recycling, global warming, organic farming, and alternative energy. Being small gives companies the advantage they need to capitalize on the inability of big corporations to respond quickly to changing consumer demands. A saying I'm hearing a lot in the business world these days is, "It takes a long time to turn the *Titanic* around." As an example, I've seen firsthand in the last year huge international fashion labels struggling with production cycles that consume a minimum of 18 months, from designing a clothing line on paper to manufacturing it abroad to delivering it to major retailers. They recognized the danger of missing fashion trends because of such a protracted production cycle and secretly worried about small start-up designers manufacturing in the United States filling the void. The same market pressures can be applied to just about any industry in the United States, meaning it's never been easier to take market share away from the big boys by designing and bringing innovative products to the marketplace while they're still trying to turn their huge, lumbering ships around. I know people in the automotive industry who are developing products and selling them direct to the big auto manufacturers who are happy to find new ways of thinking to captivate consumers and bring them back to the showroom. Having sold successfully into some of the biggest retailers in the United States myself, I know the pressure that their buyers are under to find new products to lure consumers into the stores. If you have ideas to help them do their jobs and generate revenues for their shareholders, now's the time to bring them. Don't wait another day! They're desperate and looking for a way to stimulate new sales.

Take Advantage of This Historic Opportunity

This isn't just limited to product manufacturers or retailers; you can apply these same principles to service providers, including everything from hair salons to accountants to plumbers. With so much competitive pressure on existing companies to survive, you're going to be forced to do whatever you can to set yourself apart, to think of a new way to service customers, to market yourself or to leverage your brand to take you into the future. Fortunately, a lot of these new ideas for marketing and connecting with new and existing consumers in meaningful ways are being invented through social media, which, for the most part, is free. I'll tell you how to do that later in this book.

RULE #7: THE AMERICAN $$$ BRAND

If you have to weather a recession, the best place to do it on earth is still the United States. And the best place to start a business on earth is also the United States. In fact, the best place to get a university education is the United States. And the United States is still the cultural arbiter of the world, which a record Hollywood box office in 2008 proves. If women in this country are taking their role as the most powerful cultural arbiters and social influencers in history by starting businesses in record numbers, communicating in revolutionary new ways, creating their own media, and redefining work and family roles for the benefit of all, it just follows that American women have a historic opportunity to take their social agenda beyond the borders of this great country to the world.

If entrepreneurs are the new rock stars, then the United States is the rock star country. Confidence, courage, and creativity are all part of the American persona ingrained in us from birth, which we project out for everyone else to see, making them either want to be like us or be with us. And that's a good thing; as market innovators and cultural arbiters for the world we should be busy using this time of a low dollar to figure out how to commercialize the American brand and turn one billion Chinese—who are in love with all things American—into consumers of U.S. goods. Some people have suggested that the American brand has become irrevocably tarnished by the tawdry behavior of the financial industry over the last 10 years, marking the beginning of the end of American capitalism and economic domination. I've got one thing to say to those people: You can drop 10 nuclear bombs on the United States and it won't kill free market innovation or the American $$$ brand. But don't hate us because we're beautiful. The United States is everyone—Europeans, Chinese, Africans, Mexicans, South Americans, Australians, Russians, Egyptians, Indians, Iraqis and Afghanis and Iranians and Koreans. You name it, they're here, part of the melting pot and mix of freedom and democracy and money that makes this the greatest country on the face of the earth to start a business. There's enough America for everyone to go around. The world needs you economic heroes who are taking on personal risk to start businesses in record numbers, creating the wealth and employment opportunities that will lead us out of a world recession—and they need you now!

Be the Rock Star!

Not only were more small businesses created in the United States in 2007 than at the height of the dot-com era in the late 90s, but according to census data, an average of 550,000 small businesses have been created in this country every month of every year—since 1996. The United States has the highest survival rates of new businesses, too, in fact, more than three times higher than the other countries responsible for starting the most new businesses, including Germany, Italy, Portugal, and Finland. Obviously, we must be doing something right here because some of those companies have gone on to become the world's leading corporations, including Wal-Mart and Microsoft, as well as Amazon, Yahoo!, and Google, which barely existed a decade ago. This kind of exponential growth is possible only through a potent combination of money, talent, and guts, which is found here in abundance, and not only brings immigrants from around the world to our universities every year, but makes them want to start businesses here, too. A recent study by Duke University found that 52 percent of Silicon Valley start-ups were founded by immigrants, up from around 25 percent 10 years ago. Another 25 percent of the United States' science and technology start-ups, generating $52 billion and employing 450,000 people, have had a foreign-born CEO or chief technology officer. In 2006, foreign nationals were named as inventors or co-inventors in a quarter of U.S. patent applications, up from 7.6 percent in 1998. The real star of the show might be U.S. consumers, though. It's our restless desire for something new or better or more beautiful or more functional that drives the innovation that powers the world's markets. With women influencing the demands of the consumer market in historic ways, it's time for women to add our billion-dollar companies to this list!

RULE #8: GO BIG OR GO HOME

Okay, I know this seems counterintuitive. I mean, didn't I just tell you that small was the new big? Guess what? They're both true. The best way to run a business these days when it comes to overhead is as small as possible. But that doesn't mean you shouldn't think big. Especially women, whom I find often limit the vision for their businesses out of habit or for other reasons I can't understand. Throughout my business journey I've had to regularly reteach myself to see the big picture on a yearly basis. It wasn't until I successfully raised private equity from angel investors to grow my company, at the same time recruiting world-class individuals who had a hand in either starting or growing some of the biggest businesses of the last 20 years, that I truly learned how to think big. In fact, we had one person on the team, who had helped take a famous brand from start-up to $700 million a year in sales, whom we referred to euphemistically as "Big Picture Blue Sky." He didn't even know how to turn on a computer, and forget about getting him to concentrate on everyday details. But we all realized we needed him around for the vision he saw for the company, which challenged us in evermore creative and seemingly impossible ways every day to make it a reality. Sometimes it even seemed crazy, but it worked, and we often executed this vision with nothing more than phone calls and visits to people who were always in New York. Then again, it frequently didn't work. We used to joke that he dropped million-dollar ideas out of his head on the way to the bathroom, when some people would take a lifetime trying to come up with just one. I saw him have a brain-fart one day that resulted in a multimillion dollar idea for one company he was involved in, that was so simple, so obvious, yet so brilliant, they were executing it for almost no cost the very next week. I don't think he ever looked at even one of the thousands of Excel spreadsheets I sent him, but I didn't care. I learned from him, among many other hard and invaluable lessons, that seeing the long-range possibility for any business endeavor is an art more than a science, and it frequently involves the faculties of the heart over the head.

See the Big, Sell the Big, Be the Big

Successfully practicing the art of thinking big can be accomplished with a few simple exercises. The first thing I tell women who are starting their businesses is to think big—really big. When they finally have a vision in their heads of what really big looks like for their company, I tell them to multiply that by 100. That's how big *big* is. Sometimes I see big with a high-altitude exercise, which is where the "big picture, blue sky" analogy comes in. Imagine yourself 30,000 feet about the ground, with nothing but blue skies and sunshine all around. Beneath you is a wonderful picture of your company spread out across an illuminated landscape, complete with roads that get you from the very middle of the vision to the furthest fringes where wonderful yet dimly perceived opportunity lies. If everything went right with the execution of your business vision, and not one cloud of difficulty appeared in the blue sky to cover the sun, what would the big picture of your business look like? It's not going to happen that way, but that shouldn't keep you from forming the vision. When you can see opportunity that big, you're in the same league with Big Picture Blue Sky. It doesn't matter whether you think you can realistically execute the vision or not or even if it seems crazy or foolhardy to try, that's where you should be when it comes to thinking big.

A more practical example of this can be illustrated by a discussion I just had with my 12-year-old son while writing this. He's already been exposed to the entrepreneur virus, which means I don't have to really teach him anything—he learns it all by osmosis. Kids are the most open to becoming the entrepreneurs this country so desperately needs, because they're naturally creative and haven't learned to see barriers or limitations that most adults use to make excuses for not following their dreams. Everything is still possible. He was telling me about his writing assignment for school; the title was so instinctively brilliant, so expressive of his love of skateboard culture, so finger-on-the-pulse representative of what millions of other kids like him around the world were no doubt thinking at that very moment, that I told him it was the slogan for the new company that I wanted him to form on his summer break. Within a minute he had brainstormed the name of the company, and that's where most people would stop. Thinking big required us to discuss whether the name could be trademarked and applied broadly to products and media, from skateboards to magazines to digital media to consumer products. If not, he had to think up another name, no matter how much he loved this one. You get the picture. I was challenging him to look 10 years into the future, while he was only looking at the summer. It didn't matter that he was 12 and had no money and no experience; the currency of the New Economy is ideas.

Think Small to Think Big

I know a lot of people get stuck thinking they have to be Bill Gates or Steve Jobs to think big. I know a lot of very smart and sophisticated people, including most of the financial media, who think you have to be selling nanotechnology or cloud computing in Silicon Valley to think big, too. But that's just wrong. I just proved it with the investment statistics about what "smart money" or angel investors are investing in. In fact, the number one category that angel investors and venture capitalists alike invested in 2007 was women's media, led by some of the biggest, most prestigious venture capital firms based in the heart of this high-tech real estate just outside of San Francisco—that's how big this women's revolution is! It trumped high-tech start-ups in investment dollars, even in the heart of Silicon Valley.

I learned firsthand what smart money is really looking for when investing in a start-up from the character by that name in my first book, who happens to be one of the foremost experts on private equity in the United States, having started or been a founding investor in more than 20 companies including Google, PayPal, Napster, and Inktomi—to name a few. Investors like him are just as interested in ordinary consumer products as they are in high-tech ones, though you will never read that in any of the flashy entrepreneur magazines that overflow newsstands or see pictures of those company's founders on their covers. When

73

I met him years ago, he was just making an early round investment in a company that has managed to parlay a simple three-word phrase into a brand empire, emblazoning it on t-shirts, coffee mugs, bumper stickers, hats, dog collars—you get the picture. Anybody who thought you could build a billion-dollar brand on a simple three-word phrase that happened to capture the hearts and minds of weary consumers in search of a mantra for relaxation and fun, was thinking my kind of big.

Some of my biggest regrets in business have come from a failure to think big right at the beginning. One of the biggest things anybody's got going for their company, no matter what business they're in, is intellectual property or IP. My company was valued in the millions on the basis of intellectual property alone, which includes patents, trademarks, and copyrights. Nowadays though, according to my very expensive IP attorney, a URL or web site address is the key part of intellectual property, even more important than a trademark, and it costs under $10 to register one. As for those people who sit around and come up with URL names all day, then squat on them by purchasing them while doing nothing except waiting for somebody to buy them—forget about them. I haven't bought a web site address yet from people like them. My best advice when it comes to trademarks and brands and URLs is crazy is good. Think Google, or Kleenex, or even Twitter, for that matter. URL squatters haven't been creative enough to register a web site address I want badly enough that I would be willing to buy from them yet. That's why they're squatters and why I'm running companies. There are literally an infinite number of names to choose from, so be creative and remember you sell to consumers' hearts, not their heads.

NEW ECONOMY RULE #9: THE ONLY THING WE HAVE TO FEAR IS FEAR ITSELF

I'm not one to focus on the negative, but there are certain economic realities that characterize this unique time in history that simply can't be ignored. I'm also not one of those people who thinks maintaining an unflinchingly positive attitude in the face of so much epic financial transformation going on in this country and the world as a result of mismanaged financial markets for the last 10 years, is a good thing. In fact, it borders on stupidity. This is one crisis in which positive thinking or visualizing paychecks coming to your mailbox is not going to get you through. That kind of thinking might have worked in the old economy that preceded this recent financial meltdown, but I've personally reached my bandwidth for bullshit when it comes to visualizing money entering your life as a solution.

This brings me to the acceptance of the new reality of dealing with debt. So many people are facing financial crisis as a result of events beyond their control. Either they're upside down on their home mortgages, meaning they owe more than their houses are worth as a result of plummeting real estate values, or they're faced with debt they can just no longer service because of other economic conditions outside of their control, including losing their jobs or struggling with the overhead of running businesses in this time of great change. Nothing makes me angrier than seeing the finger of blame pointed solely at consumers for this mess we're in, especially by certain financial commentators on cable networks who watched this whole train wreck happen in the financial markets without so much as a tough question directed at those executives responsible for truly immoral and unethical behaviors, who were frequently guests on their shows. When major banks have debt to asset ratios like Bank of America at 134:1, and Citibank at 88:1, and major corporations are going bankrupt around us daily as a means to rid themselves of billions of dollars of debt and escape contracts with both employees and small business vendors, why should you spend a minute agonizing over the realities of bankruptcy for yourself or your business? For these big companies, it's not a personal decision, it's a simple business decision. It's true that consumers are not without fault. There's enough blame for everyone to go around here, but the time for blame is over. New realities are forcing upon us the need for new solutions, especially when the ability to repay debt is a function of current economic conditions, such as losing your job or seeing your business receipts drop precipitously, and not your willingness to pay your bills. So in between ignoring bad news and visualizing money coming to your mailbox, take some time to deal with the fear head on, accept the defeat if that's what's called for, and move into the future with the past behind you as prologue.

Manage the Crisis

I believe educating ourselves as consumers and business-people as to the reality of the current economic climate is the first step to intelligently taking control of our destiny in it. When everything is in crisis, the law of the jungle says adapt or die.

If you already own a business, don't waste one minute wringing your hands. Take immediate action to protect it by focusing on these points.

Cash Is King

This may never have been truer than it is right now. If you have cash, protect it first, hoard it second. Don't pay out cash unless you absolutely have to until economic conditions become more stable. Barter, negotiate, and try to get new terms from your creditors, paying the minimum possible with reduced interest rates. Now is the time to negotiate, when banks are seriously overextended. Take them to the mat! You may be able to pay off lines of credit for pennies on the dollar at this unique time in history when everyone is over their heads in debt, especially the banks! They're willing to collect and take write-downs or tax credits on the money they lose, so don't feel bad about it for one minute. A lot of people are questioning what a credit rating is worth nowadays when credit is so tight that banks are not only not lending, but they're calling in loans on businesses who have excellent credit in an effort to shore up cash reserves and reduce their debt-to-asset ratios, effectively putting those businesses out of business. If the choice is between paying your loans in full on time or feeding your family, paying your employees, and keeping your dream alive, make the choice for your family, employees, and business every time.

Follow the Money

Where are your business's profit centers? Find them and focus all your energy and resources on them right now. Notice I didn't say revenues, I said profits. During these times, you can't afford to carry loss leaders or products that you sell with little or no profit just to bring customers in the door. Don't squander precious resources on unprofitable revenue streams when you can be focusing them on areas where small investments of time or money yield the highest returns. Forget the scalpel—get an ax. Don't be afraid to take dramatic action to scale back or even eliminate parts of your business that aren't producing, even if it's a core part of your business. You'll not only have more money at the end of the week, you'll sleep a lot better, too. Better yet, take the money you save and pour it into developing and growing those parts of your business that are bringing in the profits, and sell like crazy. Be fearless, when everyone else is cowering in fear.

Consider Bankruptcy

I know this is against any advice I've given previously, but desperate times call for desperate measures. If the writing's on the wall, and the prospects for saving your business are bleak, don't waste any time going bankrupt, and don't let yourself get in a position where you can't afford the legal costs of going bankrupt. There's no shame in it anymore, when even the biggest and most prestigious companies are doing it. Even Donald Trump filed for bankruptcy this year in his Atlantic City casino division. In fact, I know people in southern California who are espousing a new "bankruptcy chic"—if you don't have a story, you aren't cool. Reset your debt and start over again. It will feel like a million pounds have been lifted off your shoulders and give you the emotional and physical strength you need to survive in a new incarnation. Go see an attorney who specializes in bankruptcy and find out all your rights and responsibilities under the law. In this current economy, bankruptcy is not a personal reflection on you; it's simply a business decision based on unique financial realities. It could be the best decision you'll ever make.

The Usual Suspects

Do whatever it takes right now to get by on as little as possible. That means saying "no" to just about anyone who is trying to sell you a service you don't need or that doesn't have a demonstrable return on investment. Anything can and might happen in the next year or two so avoid long-term commitments like leases if you can. If you have a long-term lease, especially on a pricey commercial property that has drastically lost value in the last year, renegotiate it now. If there are a lot of empty spaces in your office building, you're holding a lot of leverage so use it to reduce your lease costs, especially if that's the difference between your business surviving or not. Rediscovering the age-old art of bartering is something I'm doing right now when it comes to dealing with some of my suppliers and vendors who get a lot of exposure from working with me on high-profile events. Also, there are a lot of exceptionally talented people out of jobs looking for employment. If you can bring them on in your company with the offer of an ownership share or equity position, in lieu of a salary, now's the time to do it. I've brought people on for tiny equity positions in my company with priceless, world-class experience, who have contributed significantly to my success. If you're hesitant to give away any ownership in exchange for work, particularly if it means the difference between your company surviving or thriving, ask yourself this question: Five percent of nothing is?

RULE #10: WOMEN WILL NOT BE DENIED THEIR PLACE IN THE NEW ECONOMY

This isn't a political revolution, it's an economic revolution. It isn't just a women's revolution; it's a family revolution. As I've already proven, the opportunities available in this New Economy aren't limited to high-tech industries, Wall Street, graduates of Ivy League colleges, or even U.S.-born citizens. It's not being led by politicians on a state or national level or special-interest groups lobbying in Washington; it's not being legislated, or bailed out, or proposed, or voted on, or paid for by taxpayer dollars. It's a real revolution of the people and this is its manifesto.

This Is an Equal Opportunity Economic Revolution

In fact, much of this renaissance of ideas and capital and products and opportunity is being driven not only by women, but by women of color, who are taking a historic role in staking out their claim in the economic future of this country. I know up until this point this discussion has focused on gender and not race. The fact is that as glaring as the gender inequities are for women in the top ranks of corporate America, higher education, Hollywood, Wall Street, and everywhere else, they are significantly worse for women of color, who remain almost invisible in these places. Let's make it clear right now, racial diversity is just as important as gender diversity; unfortunately, I don't have time to write that book right now. The simple, indisputable fact is that whether they are white, black, Asian, Latina, or whatever—women are dropping out of the corporate workplace in record numbers and starting businesses of their own for the same reason: to take control of their financial destinies. In fact, the growth of new businesses owned by minority women skyrocketed in 2008, growing three times faster than all other U.S. firms according to a new report from the Center for Women's Business Research.

AN EQUAL OPPORTUNITY REVOLUTION

The report "Businesses Owned by Women of Color in the United States 2008" found that firms owned by African-American, Asian, and Hispanic women "substantially outpace" all U.S. firms in terms of revenue growth and number of employees. "The face of women entrepreneurship is changing," said center Chairwoman Margaret Smith. "Today, women of color represent 26 percent of all women business owners—up from 20 percent just a few years ago. These business owners are a vital driver of economic growth in every community and a vibrant source of suppliers and customers." According to the report, between 2002 and 2008, the number of privately held firms in which women of color had at least a 50 percent stake grew 30 percent while all other businesses grew 9 percent. Not only are more minority women starting businesses, but the data shows that they are experiencing greater success doing it; revenues for minority-owned women's businesses grew 35 percent compared with 15 percent for all other firms and employment grew 22 percent compared with 2 percent for all firms. With these kinds of results, I think some of our biggest corporations that are currently facing hard times should go about finding a minority woman CEO to take over as quickly as possible!

Among the women from traditionally underrepresented groups, Latinas own the largest number of businesses, an estimated 747,108 firms, employing 430,000 workers and generating revenues of nearly $62 billion as of 2008. African-American women own the second-highest number of firms (734,664), employ 281,055 people, and have revenues of more than $32 billion. Firms owned by Asian-American women outpaced all other firms in growth in numbers, employment, and receipts. Asian-American women own the third-largest number of firms (627,837), employ 898,240 people and have revenues totaling $128 billion.

IT'S A HISTORIC TIME, AND I'M TAKING MY PLACE IN HISTORY

This isn't about creating change through the political process anymore. We're beyond that. That was the first women's revolution. In women's revolution 2.0 we're commanding power through our control of this economy to take our fair share. We're not asking anymore; we're taking. But as powerful as that is, there's something else happening that is so big, so revolutionary, so empowering, that some of the smartest, most prescient people from some of the most prestigious think tanks in the world are calling it one of the most significant social events in human history. And guess what? Women are leading this revolution, too.

CHAPTER 5

Moms Are the New Geeks

Don't look now, but we are in the midst of a revolution that may be even more powerful and transforming than any economic or technological or political revolution that's come before: It's a communication revolution. It's the ability to disseminate ideas in real time through infinite channels of communication at almost no cost. It's a stealth revolution, flying under the radar of even the experts, including those who make a living writing books and commenting in the media about social trends. Not only that, it's been overlooked by general partners at venture capital firms, and underscrutinized by gadget manufacturers, unexploited by software developers, and underreported by the serious press. Why? Because it's being led by moms, and nobody pays attention to moms. Moms just aren't sexy enough for a majority of the intelligentsia, venture capital firms, gadget manufacturers, software manufacturers, and serious press to be interested in. After all, all innovation is driven by early adopters, and everyone knows early adopters are nerdy geeks who are almost always young men in their 20s with iPhones and lots of time to spend staring at their computers' glowing screens trying out new software applications and gadget features and widgets on their multiple social networks. I mean, all this stuff is sexy, and moms are definitely not sexy! After all, it's the geeks who create the demand for the products and media and online platforms that the rest of the consumers like moms, pops, and great aunts will wake up to and buy a year or so later. Moms aren't the arbiters, they're just the consumers, right? *Wrong!*

MOMS ARE THE NEW GEEKS

Sorry geeks, but your 15 minutes of fame are up. Yes, you colonized Twitter and made it one of the fastest growing cultural phenomenons in Web 2.0, racking up record numbers of followers in just weeks and measuring your social influence in those numbers. Yes, you venture capital firms followed the siren song sung by those prescient geeks and poured millions into Twitter without even a whiff of revenues, because it was an exciting phenomenon and that's what the geeks were spending their time doing and they were prescient after all. They must know something you don't about the vision for future opportunities. Yes, you social media gurus of popular culture touted the power and influence of those geeks, telling us all to urgently care about what they were thinking and doing and tweeting and texting on their iPhones because even though they were a small group of people, they were going to change the world with that all-powerful influence of theirs. Guess what—when it comes to creating real social influence that's going to change the real world, there's a new boss in town, and that boss is mom.

BUT WHERE'S THE MONEY? SHOW ME THE MONEY

Geeks aren't social influencers; they're masters of the medium, which is the machine for communication or the vehicle for ideas. The gadgets and microblogging software platforms that geeks pour their time into and venture capitalists pour their money into and social media gurus tout are just the means, they are not the message. The medium, for example Twitter, seems impressive when you witness its exponential growth and its ability to connect millions around the world in real time chat or microblogs, but these media are becoming so ubiquitous as to become themselves mere commodities, or something that is so common as to only have value in great amounts, or to be so ever-present as to be free. Even the experts have come to that conclusion, as leading Internet analyst Jeffrey Lindsay of Sanford C. Bernstein & Co. LLC, pointed out in his recent report, "The Ruinous History of 'Pre-Business' Internet Deals," cited in a story by Richard Morgan on Reuters titled "The Trouble with Twitter," published March 20, 2009. "Whoever buys [Twitter] will likely have to operate it at a loss in perpetuity, or until the next cool Web 2.0 social networking concept comes along and Twitter tweets no more," was Lindsay's conclusion. This isn't the first time that investors have made bad investments betting on the medium instead of the message. An example of another bad deal of "spectacular proportions," according to the report, was the $120 billion valuation of AOL, which dropped precipitously to $3 billion after its merger with Time Warner, Inc.

THE FICKLE GEEK

Part of the problem, according to the same report, is that geeks are fickle. They have no loyalty and are often not motivated by profit. They randomly create open source software for people to use for free just because they can. Consequently, they're not willing to pay for anything and if forced to submit to advertising or subscription fees, they'll quickly flee to find another free platform offering the same service or make one themselves. We saw it happen in the music industry a decade ago with Napster, which started as an open source file-sharing program that allowed people to "share" music, and now struggles after the fact to become a profitable, revenue-generating medium for delivering musical content legitimately, as new free music-sharing or even listening software programs spread like wildfire across the Internet to challenge it—until someone shuts those down. It's still the distribution of the valuable content that drives the creation of the commodity of machines.

PERCEPTION IS REALITY—*Not*!

If geeks are being touted as our most important cultural arbiters by virtue of being the number one early adopters of new technology, then moms are the new geeks, because the research shows that it's moms—not geeks—that are the new number one early adopters of new technology.

That's according to a new study by Solutions Research Group (SRG), a Toronto-based research firm, among other studies. Donna Hall, senior director with SRG, says that when it comes to new media and gadget use in our daily lives, women have surged ahead of men in virtually every category. Whether it's gadgets like cell phones and digital cameras, or media like streaming video, social networking, digital video recorders (DVRs), and casual gaming, women are using them more than men, and consequently driving real market innovation through that mastery and demand for two reasons: to save time and to connect with each other.

TIME-SHIFTERS

Everybody knows moms are the busiest people on earth. As a result, nobody's got a greater need to time shift than moms. Time-shifting is the process of recording TV shows on a DVR for viewing at a more convenient time, and nobody's doing it more than women. Hall estimates that busy moms challenged to balance career and family are creating an average of 15 minutes of found time per hour of TV programming by fast-forwarding through commercials on shows they have recorded. Her study found that when there is a DVR in the household, women exceed men in terms of weekly usage—9.3 times per week versus 8.3 for men. The majority of women with DVRs watch at least as much recorded programming as live. And they watch the recorded show fairly quickly after the original show has aired, typically later the same evening or the next day. "We often hear women in focus group discussions saying that they watch more TV since getting a DVR," says Hall.

According to Hall, women also watch more TV streamed over the Internet from network sites like ABC, CBS, and Fox, though, with the exception of college-age women, they can't be bothered to download movies or TV shows from peer-to-peer sites, which men are more likely to do.

GAMING

It's hard to believe that women are overtaking men in the PC gaming market, but the same study by SRG confirms that this market for women is growing rapidly. Even handheld game units like Nintendo DS and Sony PSP are becoming very popular with women, who are using them to fend off boredom during commuting times or when traveling. According to SRG data, 70 percent of all women played a PC game in the last month, visiting free online games sites or playing games such as solitaire, "The Sims," "Bejeweled," or "Mahjong." And women are playing more console games as well: 38 percent play console games, up from 35 percent one year ago. Among teen girls and young adults 12 to 24, 69 percent play console games. This underserved market is so wide open with opportunity for developing games around women, that if I knew the first thing about it I would be in this business tomorrow. Somebody jump on it!

GADGETS

Research that shows that women upload more photos from their digital cameras to their PCs than men testifies again to the fact that women are the consumers driving innovation in the digital camera market through the mastery and use of this technology. Though digital cameras were the number one gadget that women bought between December of 2007 and February of 2008, cell phones came in a close second. Most of the cell phone purchases were upgrades to newer state-of-the-art smartphones, and the features most in demand were those that give women the ability to capture video while also allowing them to upload or provide direct links to that video on their social networks, including MySpace or Facebook. Coming in third on the list of gadgets that women are buying are console/handheld games, followed by laptops and digital media players. What was important to the women consumers in this study was that all these technologies were not only portable and easy to use, but that they brought greater enjoyment and ease in their lives by allowing them to facilitate social connections.

WEB USERS

But women are not only time-shifting and adopting the newest gadgets more than men, they are also surfing the Web more than men, according to Horizon Media Senior VP of Research Brad Adgate. Adgate concludes that this new breed of mom is an educated multitasker between the ages of 18 and 39, who is "very adept with technology," surfing the Web an average of 87 minutes a day and communicating about online and product experiences via e-mail, smartphone, and their own blogs. This communicating is precisely where real social influence is being created on everything from consumer products and parenting to business, education, entertainment, and everything under the sun—the exchange of opinions between moms in real time. Their willingness to pioneer social networking, connect, and discuss everything—not just high-tech gadgets or new software platforms—transcends by far any breadth of social influence controlled by that small slice of demographic that belongs to the classically defined geek. The explosion of connections and communication between women via "mommy blogs" showed a growth of 35 percent last year alone, faster than every other category on the Web except politics, according to comScore, an Internet traffic measurement company. In comparison, comScore does not even track men's sites as a category.

SUPER CONSUMERS

Marketers are becoming increasingly aware of the power of this new breed of moms who are plugged in and whose opinions are trusted by their peers. Consequently, advertisers are spending big dollars to connect with these new super consumers, serving up 4.4 billion display ads on women's web sites in May of 2008 alone, according to comScore. "Moms are the decision makers of the household as far as purchases are concerned," said Chris Actis, VP and digital director at the advertising agency Media Vest. This explosion of traffic and advertising on sites geared to women has also radically reshaped the media business in the last two years, while attracting millions of dollars of investment from venture capital firms, including some based in Silicon Valley, where investment in women's media overtook all other business start-ups, including high-tech, in 2007. "I love women," said Tim

Draper, co-founder and managing director of Draper Fisher Jurvetson, a major Silicon Valley venture capital firm, explaining his firm's heavy investment in Glam Media, rumored, in 2008, to be the fastest growing start-up in history. "Women are more than half the population, and they do most of the shopping." Finally! Somebody gets it! We're powerful. We're not just buying shoes. But for most brands that were primarily marketing to men until this explosion in 2008, it's been a game of catch-up to respond to this tidal wave of female early adopters. "Brands that market to men, like car and technology companies, were the first to feel comfortable advertising online," said Chas Edwards, chief revenue officer and publisher at Federated Media in a *New York Times* article in August 2008 titled "Woman to Woman, Online." Oops—guess he must not have gotten the memo that said that women are the number one early adopters of technology, not men. And a recent study done by the automotive industry found that women are the chief decision makers when it comes to buying cars, responsible for 68 percent of all new vehicle purchases and 65 percent of all tire purchases. Analyst Bruce Leichtman, president of Leichtman Research Group, in a February 2008 *Television Week* article analyzing gender-related viewing differences, predicted that between time-shifting and online viewing, women television viewers will force a sea-change in the television industry in the coming years. The problem, he points out, is that for the first time, advertisers and the agencies that sell the ads will be unable to quantify how many eyeballs are actually seeing the ads and how many are just fast-forwarding through them. Describing the dilemma that companies like Nielsen, the media research company that conducts audience measurement, are facing, Leichtman said: "New media and time-shifting are taking away a considerable amount of inventory we can quantify via Nielsen. Using the word 'dire' is dramatic but not off base."

NEW MEDIA

But the explosion of women online has not only radically reshaped the advertising industry, while also driving product innovation, it's also simultaneously revolutionized all forms of media, from print to television. Perhaps nowhere is that more clear than with regard to new media. Even the definition of what exactly new media is changes daily. When I started my media company in January of 2008, some people were still calling new media "digital media," two words that I rarely hear together anymore. Now I hardly even hear the words "new media" used anymore. "Social media" is replacing "new media" as quickly as it replaced "digital media." Let me make it clear—social media is just a new component of new media; social media is the conversation while new media is the content. This is a quickly evolving landscape, a Wild West frontier where the words, rules, and the players change in epic ways every day. The upstart little guys have just as good a chance of cashing in big as do those New York- and Los Angeles-based flagship media and advertising companies that are furiously trying to turn their titanic-sized ships around in time to maneuver to new opportunities. In short, this is just one of those historic new opportunities for creating wealth in the New Economy. Oh, and if you haven't noticed already by virtue of all this exhaustive research, in addition to women being the new geeks, they're also the new media moguls.

NEW MEDIA MOGULS

Not only is innovation powered by women early adopters creating new products, but it's also the driving force behind the creation of revolutionary new business models in the media business. Women are not only rewriting the way media, particularly TV, gets consumed, they are also redefining what content gets produced. Not satisfied to be simply media consumers anymore, almost every woman I know is involved in some way in creating her own media every day, whether it's via a blog, uploaded videos to YouTube, podcasts, newsletters, even elaborately decorated and flared out MySpace and Facebook pages—and the list doesn't end there. Some women are turning their personal lifestyles into media empires including video blogs or vlogs, merchandise, advertising, and even TV and book deals. The women who are the most successful at creating the new types of content that women are flocking to read are creating outside the box, particularly the TV box. Whether recounting in pictures, videos, and words the homespun lifestyle of a mom who crafts and homeschools her children in rural Maine; or documenting a more irreverent and humorous take on motherhood in the midst of chaos; it's obvious that women are seeking and tuning in daily to the voices of other women who are offering alternative views into their unconventional lives. Even traditional magazines are feeling the pressures, trading in slick paper editions for online versions, complete with web TV shorts on their print stories. At the same time that Hollywood is struggling to capitalize on this historic opportunity, looking for ways to transition its traditional episodic shows to the Web, a hundred new upstart production companies from Silicon Valley to Austin to any town across the United States are redefining what episodic TV shows look like by producing all kinds of new short formats created especially for the Web, featuring the kind of content women haven't seen before in traditional media sources. One thing's for sure, with corporations eager to capture the eyeballs of today's new superconsumers, advertisers and content creators alike are rushing to set up shop on whatever medium today's moms watch, wherever they watch it—whether it's TV, DVRs, the Web, or even their smartphones.

SOCIAL MEDIA

I have seen the future of media, and it is social and run by women. That's not just my opinion, that's the opinion of a recent study by Rapleaf, a company that provides research on search and social networking, reported in *Business-Week* in May 2008 by Auren Hoffman in a story titled "The Social Media Gender Gap." The study found that when it came to social media, women are again at the forefront as early adopters, far outpacing men in sheer numbers. The social media landscape is changing so quickly, it's hard to pin down a precise definition of it, but it can be explained generally as any primarily Internet-based application that allows people to create or maintain relationships with each other while communicating in myriad ways in a virtual environment. Some of the oldest and most popular social media platforms are MySpace, Facebook, and LinkedIn, with Twitter and Ning seeing exponential growth in the last year. But that doesn't even begin to scratch the surface of what's out there now, and what's currently being developed for tomorrow. I'll spend the next chapter going into specifics on each, but for now, what's important to remember is that it's women's desire for social interaction with each other that is driving this phenomenon of innovation in both medium and content.

The Rapleaf study looked at the social media habits of 13.2 million people. Its conclusion was that not only do more women than men currently use social media, but the next wave of innovation will likely target women, widening the user gender gap even more. In fact, the study concludes that if you're going to create a new web site and you want it to go viral, or become wildly popular, you'd better target women. Specifically, it found that among twenty-somethings, women and men were just as likely to be members of social networks, but the women were much more active than the men. Men above age 30, particularly married men, aren't even joining social networks (with the exception of LinkedIn) in large numbers, and if they do, they're typically not hanging out there. In comparison, married women are joining social networks in droves, with women between the ages of 35 and 50 making up the fastest growing segment. The study found that an explanation for the disparity between genders comes down to this: Men are transactional and women are social. Men tend to look at social interactions online as more of a business relationship that yields a desired effect, whether it's helping them make connections for their job, purchase something, or provide them with the information they're looking for on news, sports, or financial markets. Women, on the other hand, go online primarily for the personal relationships, including communicating with friends, posting pictures and videos of family, or finding other niches of support or friendship. Women use social networks to get information, too, but the information they rely on most of the time comes from their friends or peers in their social network, a phenomenon being called "conversational marketing" by the advertising industry. The Pew Internet & American Life Project reports that 85 percent of online users in the United States have received help from their online network when making a big decision. They call this "networked individualism," and suggest that people get advice from friends and others from their social networks. Therefore, many marketers and advertisers are realizing that every dollar spent marketing to women has a much wider return on investment than that same dollar spent advertising to men. How social media mania will continue to reshape the future of media as a whole is something that nobody knows for sure right now. The only certainty is that women are in the driver's seat.*

SHOW ME THE WOMEN

I was unable to find up-to-date specifics on the number of women who currently occupy brand management positions in major corporations in the United States or even have executive-level positions in top advertising agencies, but according to the article "The Social Media Gender Gap" in *BusinessWeek* in May of 2008, most large corporations employ male brand managers. Getting up-to-date data on the percentages of women being hired for social media positions in corporations or even as consultants would be challenging if not impossible at this time. In my own observations on the front lines of this rapidly changing business frontier, I see more men than women being identified

*Find more data from the RapLeaf study at www.rapleaf.com/company_press_2007_11_12.html.

as leaders or experts in the emerging billion–dollar social media industry. If women are running this show, driving both the innovation of the platforms and the content of social media, while also representing 75 percent of all consumer purchases and a demographic advertisers are desperate to reach via social media, we should see more women than men in executive positions at the top of corporations and advertising agencies in the social media departments, and we should see them now. Perhaps we can use our social influence to tell advertisers what we want—with our voices and our pocketbooks. But then again, maybe we can just buy our own products direct from each other—Buy Mom!

THE MOBILE WEB

What happens when you put gadgets, gaming, time-shifting, web-surfing, blogging, and social networking together in one place? You get the mobile Web via today's new smartphones. What happens when you put those smartphones in the hands of today's number one early adopters of all these new technologies—moms? You get the most powerful, plugged-in consumers and social influencers in history. What do you get when you add in all the new technological and communication factors that some of the smartest people in the United States are calling the biggest social and economic event in history?

WOMEN TAKING OVER THE WORLD

As big as all this is, prepare to have your mind blown. Everything up to this point has prepared us for this moment in history where technology and communication come together to empower people—particularly women—in ways that are beyond revolutionary, that could literally change the course of history not just in the United States, but the world.

We're in the midst of a wireless revolution, the sheer numbers and exponential growth of which dwarf anything we've seen before in terms of technology and the benefits that come from our adaptation of it including information, knowledge, communication, and commerce. It's the mobile Web. It's the ability to stream extraordinary amounts of information through broadband technology including data, voice, and video, wherever and whenever we want it via smartphones. It's the ability to share that same information and communicate in real time with people all over the world through infinite channels of communication at almost no cost. It's the ability for women, who are leading this revolution on all fronts, to take a message of peace and love to the world.

THE BIGGEST TECHNOLOGICAL AND SOCIAL EVENT IN OUR LIFETIMES

Broadband technology is an emerging technology, evolving in size, penetration, and cost; it is a high-speed, high-capacity transmission medium that carries information from multiple independent network carriers through different bandwidth channels, supporting data, voice, and video over long distances simultaneously. The introduction of broadband technology is what is powering innovation in the market for smartphones, that new breed of phones including BlackBerrys, Pres, and iPhones, that transcend the normal definition of a cell phone by adding advanced

98

capabilities like web browsing, text messaging, streaming video, and social networking platforms, to name a few. In a nutshell, it brings more information to users at a faster speed with greater capacities by increasing the ability to transmit data through increased bandwidth. In order to appreciate how significant this technological trend is in terms of size and growth, you need to compare it to statistics on what has come before.

The introduction of the first personal computer, ushering in the PC age as we know it, happened just over 25 years ago. It's estimated that there are currently 1 billion personal computers in use in the world right now. Broadband technology is a relative newcomer, only becoming commercially available to consumers in a significant way in the last five years. There are currently 3 billion handsets or smartphones in use in the world today, three times the number of personal computers in only one-fifth the time. Not only that, we're adding 500 million more smartphone users a year to that 3 billion, with that number expected to grow exponentially as the technology, price, and availability of both the phones and the broadband network of services grow, making them more widely available to people all over the world. According to Glen Hutchins, president of Silver Lake, a leading venture capital firm investing in emerging technologies, "This reach is really unprecedented. There is no new technology in history that has reached so many people so broadly dispersed around the world so quickly. The economic activity this generates is enormous." That was his conclusion in an address to leading economic and political leaders in Washington, D.C., and televised on C-Span in August of 2008. This is one of the reasons vast amounts of money are being poured into building the infrastructure of the broadband network in the

United States by President Obama as part of the economic stimulus package. The economic opportunity inherent in building the networks, making the equipment to support it, manufacturing the smartphones, developing the operating systems for the phones including the software, employing the people to service the networks and the billions of users, as well as the creation of new content for those billions of users, constitutes, according to Hutchins, *"enormous, enormous* economic activities that dwarf anything we've seen in our lifetimes." Let's make sure we take our share.

IT'S A HISTORIC TIME

Let's take our place in history. Forget about all the talk of doom and gloom. Everything is changing. Don't confuse change with fear. Old institutions are failing, but in their place new and better ones are being created. Barriers to entry are falling in the world of business in an epic fashion everywhere I look. We're simultaneously in the midst of major technological advances that will change our lives in this country and around the world for the better. People will be empowered in unique and exciting ways through unprecedented access to information and communication as well as channels of distribution. Beyond the historic economic opportunity lies the social benefits that will come from giving more than a billion people a voice along with the platform to communicate with each other in real time for purposes of commerce, social networking, or maybe even more important, issues of peace and sustainability. It is a movement that has never been seen before in human history, and women are poised to take their place as leaders on this world stage.

CHAPTER 6

A New Society

"We become what we behold."
—Marshall McLuhan

If a society is defined as a group of people organized politically and economically and sharing a distinct cultural identity with the ability to communicate that identity, then we're on the verge of a new society. We're already remaking American society economically, and now with the unprecedented phenomenon of immediate mass communication, combined with the explosive growth of social networking platforms, a whole new society is being created. Except this new society, for the first time in history, transcends the borders of countries, socio-economic backgrounds, and even languages. This new society that is rapidly being created is global. This is demonstrated daily in my online social network community at www.mommymillionaire.com. What I've discovered is that, wherever you live—whether it's the United States, Korea, Australia, France, Israel, South Africa, or any country on earth—we all share the same dream and are using the unique opportunities available at this moment in history to make it happen. We seek control of our own financial destinies, without compromising that which is most important to us, our families. Part of what is making this possible are these revolutionary new tools of communication, which allow you to learn invaluable new information to help you succeed on everything from how to source manufacturing, contract professional services, sell your goods or services, market yourself, and turn your dream of financial independence into reality.

THE GLOBAL GOOD

These tools are just an overview of what's available out there to help you join this global society and take your place in creating the life of your dreams at this historic time. New ones are being created every day at a dizzying pace. Don't get overwhelmed. Don't try and master them all. No matter what anybody tells you right now, there are no certain rules governing the use of these tools. This is a new world where the only thing certain is change, on an almost daily basis. Again, the tools are just the medium—they're not the message. The mediums will come and go, evolve, multiply to the point of being ubiquitous, and likely remain as free as air. They're all trying to compete for your attention now, and it's some people's job to tell you that you urgently need them, but resist that pressure and stay focused on those that actually bring you measurable benefits, whether it's in friendship, commerce, networking, entertainment, support, or business. Take the ones you like, and leave the rest. I only have one hard and fast rule for success: Conduct yourself in these virtual social environments exactly as you would if you were a guest in my home. After all, the first word in "social networking" is "social." If we're going to use these tools to create a new global society, let's make sure it's civil. Let's found it on guiding principles of respect, support, kindness, and courtesy.

WOMEN ARE FROM VENUS, MEN ARE FROM MARS

I can't begin this discussion without pointing out a fact I stated previously when it comes to the way men and women interact on the Web in virtual social environments. Men are transactional and women are relational. Men typically are more pragmatic, treating online interactions as business relationships for the purpose of yielding a desired result. Women, on the other hand, use social media primarily to foster and develop relationships, whether they're personal or business. Even in strictly business environments, women expect greater levels of formal social interaction than men. So it's a given that all those rules of social etiquette you've learned that help you successfully navigate relationships and life in the real world are the basis for interaction online, because that's how you're going to be judged by your peers online. Just like in the real world, the most precious thing you have is your integrity, and all you need to do is compromise it once to lose it forever. I know it's easy to forget you're interacting with real human beings online. I've done it myself. And I've also discovered that for the most part, what is said on the Web, stays on the web—indefinitely. Who knows where you're going to be in five years; I've heard rumors this year of employment background checks including views of your Facebook page. Just know that it's a big world out there—be careful.

YOU'RE IN THE MEDIA BUSINESS NOW

Whether you're using your social networks for business or pleasure, you're in the media business now. Whether sharing photos, uploading videos, microblogging, chatting in networks, or sharing music, there are a hundred new tools that will help you create and present the multimedia expression of you or your business online. You should determine right up front whether the online social persona you're going to either launch or develop with these tools is primarily for business or personal purposes. There are certain rules of engagement that apply to either use, which are not necessarily compatible. I'll go through them in greater detail below. They are changing in dramatic ways daily, so for greater detail on how to use each one of these particular platforms, visit www.mommymillionaire.com, where you can access links or even download manuals.

TWITTER

Twitter is the newest and hottest phenomenon in social media. Characterized as a microblogging service, it allows people to send status updates of 140 characters or less known as "tweets" in answer to the question "what are you doing?" Much ado has been made about Twitter, and it has struggled to grow in response to its phenomenal popularity after launching without a revenue model in place, even breaking down occasionally under the pressure of too many tweets. Twitter is not the only microblogging service on the Web, but it is the most popular, and though it continues to look for ways to commercialize its success while managing its exponential growth, a thousand other start-ups have found a way to piggyback on Twitter's success and make money where it seems that Twitter cannot.

Twitter is currently free to join, and I would suggest that everybody who reads this book do so, if for no other reason than to see what it's all about. You simply sign up by creating an identity that can be your name, your business name, or an alias, and you're free to start tweeting. If you want people to follow you, it is in your best interest to personalize your profile with a photo and a short bio—140 characters or fewer—and trick it out a little with a custom background and colors, which you can find under the "settings" tab of your profile. You can use your own photo files to create a custom background for your Twitter profile, or you can download one free from one of the many locations on the Web that provide them like www.mytweetspace.com, where you can also add additional customization features like badges and company logos to your profile. But before you actually commit to tweeting yourself, I would recommend listening in on the Public Timeline of Twitter displayed as "Everyone" on the home tab of your profile. This is a stream of tweets from everybody around the world using Twitter at that moment, and it will help you to see what all the excitement is about. You'll see predominately English tweets, but also Chinese, Spanish, French, and other languages fly by, on every subject in the world including science, religion, politics, news, celebrity gossip, technology, social media, finance, pets, parenting—everything under the sun! If you see a tweet that interests you, you can click on the photo of the "tweeter" on the left of the timeline and be redirected to her profile page; there you can read her short bio and all her previous tweets, and even look at tweets she's selected herself as "favorites," whether they were her own tweets or those of others. If you find yourself intrigued, just click the individual's "follow" button underneath her photo, and the next time you log in, you'll see her tweets stream along with all those others you select to follow specifically under your Home tab. (Make sure you follow me at www.twitter.com/mommymillionair, as well as www.twitter.com/kimlavine and www.twitter.com/buymom.) It is my recommendation that you begin by following at least 20 people, which you can do by selecting them from the public timeline, or looking down the "following" list of somebody you have selected to see if anyone looks interesting to you. You can also search people on Twitter by importing your e-mail address book, but if you don't know the e-mail address they're using for their Twitter account, you'll more than likely have to know their alias rather than their real name to find them. As I'm writing this book, Twitter is rolling out a new search function at www.search.twitter.com, designed to compete with Google search, which allows you to search topics of interest via keywords and allows you to see tweets in real time about topics containing those keywords from people all over the world, some of whom you might be interested in following. In addition, there are many additional services that exist outside of Twitter that help you find the kind of people who are interested in the same subjects you are, which you can find listed online at www.mommymillionaire.com.

There are almost as many different ways to use Twitter as there are people, and I could write a whole book on that, but my advice now is to just jump in and learn, have fun, and see what direction it takes you. The only absolute rule you need to remember at the beginning is how to respond to someone's tweet with a tweet of your own. That in a nutshell is the whole attraction of Twitter: the ability to have a real time conversation with anyone in the world, in 140 characters or fewer, even if you and that person have never met. To respond to a tweet, begin yours with the @ sign followed by the user's name, for example @KimLavine, which automatically creates a hyperlink to that person's profile on Twitter. That way, if the person you've responded to doesn't happen to see your response on the timeline, she can find it later on the @replies tab on her profile. Many times you'll get a response to your original tweet hours if not days later, so not every conversation is held in real time. If you're feeling adventurous, I would suggest you sign up for Tweet-Deck at www.tweetdeck.com, which is another of more than a dozen free services out there that help you manage your Twitter account, with all kinds of fun functionalities, including the ability to put your tweet stream in a little column on your desktop, displaying the most up-to-the-minute tweets of those who you follow.

One of the first questions I get from new users is, "Do I have to put these tweets on my phone and how much is that going to cost?!" The answer is no, you don't have to receive tweets (which can be displayed on various applications you can download or as text messages) on your cell phone or smartphone unless you want to. Of course, if you are following a lot of people this could become very expensive very quickly if you don't have unlimited text messaging. That, or it will drive you crazy in short order. When you are creating your Twitter profile, you will have an option to set up your smartphone to receive tweets under the Settings tab on your profile. I have never done this and never will. I use a smartphone and thus have the option to use the mobile Web to check my Twitter account whenever I want, including the public timeline, the timeline of people I'm following, and any @replies I've received since the last time I checked. I also have the ability via the mobile Web to post updates to my status from my smartphone, which I often do, though people I know who have BlackBerrys use an application called TwitterBerry or Tweetie for iPhones—it's endless! If there are a couple of followers who you really want to follow above everyone else, getting updated the minute they tweet, you can subscribe to their tweets via an RSS feed, available on their profile page under the photos of people they follow. The feed will deliver just their tweets to your smartphone or e-mail box through a feed reader like Feedburner (www.feedburner.com) or Google Reader (www.google.com/reader). Just don't get overwhelmed, take it slow, have fun, and follow these few basic rules until you find the use for Twitter that best suits your needs.

THE GOOD TWITTERER

The Twitterverse is informally policed by a number of experts who regularly pass along tips on how to become a good citizen by following proper Twitter etiquette. Some of these people are on the "Top 100" Twitter user list, which you can view at sites such as www.twitterholic.com or www.twitter.grader.com/. More than likely, once you sign up, one of them will follow you, which is a good thing. They will frequently take new users under their wings and direct you to links for videos that show you how to use Twitter effectively or point you to manuals you can download on how to create an effective marketing presence using Twitter. Don't take it personally if they correct you publicly, just say "thank you," and go on your way knowing that they took time out to help you become successful. Feel free to create the Twitter persona you want; in general, the rules are simple. Twitter is in essence a conversation forum, so you are expected to engage in conversation, which means responding to @replies from your followers, as well as tweeting your own @replies to those you follow. Extra courtesy and respect go a long way in creating the warmth that sometimes is missing in interactions on the Internet, so make sure to use them generously, and always express gratitude if someone sends along information or a link that helps you. Of course, this is also a blogging platform, albeit a micro one, so intriguing statements of fewer than 140 characters that summarize an experience, thought, or mood you're in are also fair game. Some of the funniest, most popular people on Twitter rarely engage in conversation with @replies, but that's okay because everyone just wants to hear their original or humorous points of view. You can find a sampling of these people and decide if you want to follow them at www.besttweets.com, where a daily variety of one person's choice of best tweets each day is streamed. Besides conversation and microblogging, the other, and in my opinion, best reason to use Twitter is to tap into the huge amount of information that passes through the Twittersphere every minute of every day, whether it's links to news stories, business tips, parenting advice, recipes, humorous videos on YouTube, photos—everything in the world that's fit to tweet, including a lot that's not! Most of this information comes from traditional news sources like the *New York Times*, or NPR, or the *Wall Street Journal*, which you can follow to get breaking news in real time. Some of the professional Twitterers do nothing but comb the headlines of all the world's major news sources all day and tweet their picks about what's interesting and worth a read, depending on their specialty. I depend on people like this that I follow to keep me in the loop on news stories I don't have time to find on my own by scouring the Web. When one of these stories comes across your Twitter stream, and you find it interesting and worth sharing, whether it's a serious news story or a funny video, it is polite and customary to retweet it, which redistributes the tweet to your pool of followers, while acknowledging the source from whom you got it. To retweet, just copy the post and place the letters RT in front of it with a space between the @name of the original tweeter, who will later see the retweet in his or her @replies. Retweets are a way to say thank you to the person who spent time finding that information and freely sharing it with you. If someone retweets one of your tweets, it's appropriate to thank them, but don't expect personal thanks from every one of the people with tens of thousands of followers because they're being retweeted all the time and your retweet is thanks enough.

I've heard what makes a good Twitterer described by using a cocktail party analogy: Nobody is interested in listening to someone at a party who just talks and doesn't listen or reply or if they don't have anything interesting to say. So if you want to get the most out of Twitter, try to evenly divide your time between sharing interesting insights about your life or thoughts, engaging in conversation with your followers, and passing along good information or links that come your way through tweets or retweets.

TO FOLLOW OR NOT TO FOLLOW

Many people on Twitter measure their social influence by the number of followers they have, and as a result are on a never-ending quest to add hundreds if not thousands of new followers to their count every day! You will be amazed by a few people on Twitter who amassed huge numbers of followers as early colonizers of the platform, but have nothing interesting to say. Sometimes called the Twitter celebrities, they're quickly being replaced on the top 100 list by real celebrities from the original media—television. As a result, there is incredible pressure on regular users to succumb to the popularity contest that dominates all social media platforms in terms of "friend" counts. In response, Twitter recently instituted some limits on the number of friends a person can have or attempt to accumulate in one day, and if you become too aggressive in courting followers you could have your account suspended temporarily or indefinitely. Don't cave in to this pressure. This is not a popularity contest. This is Twitter after all, where a friend means nothing more than a number to a lot of people. On the other hand, most people post an average of three to four tweets a day, so even if you follow a thousand people, that really isn't a lot. Nobody reads every tweet anyway. Most people just check in throughout the day and catch what's coming by at that particular moment. There are people who have tens if not hundreds of thousands of followers who do have real social influence and who are making a lot of money doing it. This is where the rules change. If you're using Twitter for personal reasons, stick with small numbers of followers; for business reasons, go big.

Conventional wisdom on Twitter says that you should automatically follow anyone who follows you, but I would vehemently disagree with this, especially for women. There are some people out there who are up to no good, and you don't want to be associated with them. You can always tell what a person is like by the company they keep; that's why I manage my social connections very carefully, even in the digital world. I don't want my name to be associated with these people even indirectly. Some people are willing to overlook unsavory "friends" in favor of a high follower count. That's just silly. But if you want to be one of them, you can use the service Tweet Later at www.tweetlater.com, which will automatically add you as a follower to anyone who follows you, while also deleting you as a follower from anyone who decides to do the same to you. People "unfollowing" you happens all the time on Twitter; in fact, some people employ it as a strategy, unfollowing you, then refollowing you later so they can get placed higher up on your list of followers, where more people may see them and follow them, too. That, or they're trying to make themselves look more popular than they are by displaying higher follower counts compared to those they follow. I told you this was silly! Don't take it personally, it's just Twitter, where there is a lot of naked ambition on display for all the world to see on a daily basis.

On the other hand, there is nothing worse than a Twitter snob, or someone who doesn't follow a reasonable portion of their followers. These people are all over the Twitterverse, and many of them are the ones who call themselves "social media experts," which defies logic to me. A lot of new users feel pressured to follow these people because, after all, everyone else does, or because when you sign up for your account they are automatically recommended to you. My advice is to follow everyone who follows you as a matter of courtesy, provided they're not objectionable in character. This is a conversation forum, and you came to listen, if not talk. Hearing what people from all walks of life have to say about life in this amazing world of ours is one of the amazing things about being alive at this moment of history. Don't pass it up because you're just interested in the sound of your own voice. On the downside, however, you'll find a portion of these people are spammers, or people who constantly tweet the same self-interested things over and over again, in an attempt to get you to buy something or visit their web site or something else that they make money at. Unfollow them, or if you don't want to see your own follower count drop as a result—told you this was silly—you can use Twitter-Snooze www.twittersnooze.com to silence their relentless tweeting for up to 30 days at a crack without unfollowing them.

Don't fool yourself; creating and maintaining a professional presence on Twitter with tens of thousands of followers is a full-time job and I honestly don't know anyone who is truly focused primarily on their business who is doing this full-time. In other words, those who can, do, and those who are devoting themselves full-time to tweeting are calling themselves social media experts. You're going to need a calculator to keep track of the people calling themselves social media gurus on Twitter, where it seems the only criteria for becoming one is a lot of available time on your hands and an ambition to amass large number of followers through an aggressive acquisition strategy that has little emphasis on the "social" part of networking. That's why I question the real value of the social influence these people claim to command as they tweet about their waits in lines to get on planes or to speak at conferences: Are they truly shaping buying decisions or effecting meaningful social change, which is where social influence really gets demonstrated, or are they just herding cats?

TWITTER DO'S AND DON'TS

- Twitter can be highly addictive when you first get started. I call it "candy for the brain." You can easily find hours flying by and for that reason I suggest you limit your use, especially at work. This too, will pass.

- I personally can't believe some of the tweets I've read from people, some of whom I know personally, who share embarrassing insights into their personal lives or inappropriate comments about their workplace. There are a hundred anecdotal stories you can read on Twitter about people who lost their jobs, friends, prospective sales, or even radio interviews as a result. What you say can be read by anybody, anytime, anywhere—unless you protect your updates for private viewing—so keep that in mind before you tweet.

- Don't send any *automatic* Direct Messages (DMs) to anyone. Some people who use some of these extra services listed previously set up their accounts to automatically send DMs to acknowledge new followers. This practice is generally despised by Twitter users.

- Don't believe all the hype! Sometimes it seems like a large portion of the conversation on Twitter is about Twitter itself.

THIRD-PARTY APPLICATIONS

Since you can only post 140 characters or fewer at a time on Twitter you need to master the art of brevity. This is just a small sampling of free third-party applications that help you post videos, photos, and links to long URLs; new ones are being created in exponential numbers every day. The good news is that you can also use these same applications in all your other social networking platforms, so mastering them early on is not only easy but recommended.

- Twitpic (www.twitpic.com): Post a photo from your phone or the Web via Twitpic and it will automatically add it as an update to your Twitter profile, complete with any comments you or others make on it.

- Tinyurl (www.tinyurl.com) and bit.ly (www.bit.ly/): These are services that will take a long URL, an address for a web page on the Internet, and turn it into a short one, allowing you to post it without exceeding your character limit. In fact, Twitter will automatically convert most URLs you enter into shortened URLs when you post, but sometimes it's best to do it on your own first, especially if you're struggling to get it all in under 140 characters.

- Blip (www.blip.fm): This is an online music service that streams your choice of songs via your own DJ profile. Sounds complicated but it isn't. Just search a song from the exhaustive library, add it to your playlist, and post the link to it on Twitter. Next thing you know, people from around the world are listening to and commenting on your musical choices. But even this service is changing daily as musical artists are pulling their songs from the available playlists, proving once again that content is still king and up-start companies are attempting to use someone else's valuable content to build their own revenue models around.

- Flickr (www.flickr.com): This is an image and video hosting web site that allows you to share links to individual photos or entire albums of photos, complete with written blog-like commentary if you want.

There is so much more to learn, and it's evolving every day, so stop by www.mommymillionaire.com to see what the latest news and tools are, then just get involved and see where it leads you.

FACEBOOK

There are supposedly 175 million users on Facebook, (www.facebook.com) and I'm one of them. (You can find me there as Kim Lavine; please add me as a friend.) This is the social media platform that most of my friends, both real and social network friends, use to connect on a more personal level, posting photos and videos of their kids, along with regular status updates that answer the question, "What are you doing?" Facebook has recently instituted many changes, which are continuing on a daily basis, in an effort to compete with the lure of Twitter, including creating a Twitter-like stream where you can view all your friends' status updates as well as their posted items like videos, photos, and links, and add your comments. Not only that, you can set your Facebook page up so that you can update your status via Twitter, keeping your social network management to a minimum. This is especially useful if you want to share links to videos, photos, and news stories simultaneously with both your Facebook friends and Twitter followers. I only recommend this, however, for people who aren't using Twitter for conversation using @replies to their followers, which just gets to be a big mess on Facebook. Facebook can be as big or little as you want it to, and I've deliberately tried to keep my profile low when it comes to this platform, but that doesn't mean you should. There are thousands of groups and causes you can become a part of where you can connect with and get to know people from all over the world, hundreds of third-party applications you can add to your page including games, personality tests, and gadgets, and uncountable selections of "flare" such as badges, tattoos, and decorations you can use to personalize your page even more. I'm going to warn you that some of these third-party applications are nothing less than spammers trying to get your e-mail address, so use caution downloading them to your Facebook page or responding to their invitations from people you supposedly know. There is also a real-time chat function you can use to talk with friends who are online at the same time that you are. Again, the question comes down to whether you're going to use this for business or personal use—or both.

Books have been written about how to use Facebook effectively, so I'm just going to give you the basics here. Like Twitter, some people subscribe to the make-as-many-friends-as-possible philosophy, which means adding as a friend anybody who is remotely connected to you, such as a friend of a friend, and then friends of their friends, and so on. I'm not one of those people, however, it does seem to be an effective way to network for some people, taking their message or awareness of their business around the world in record time at no cost other than their time. In the world of social networking, a "friend" has a whole different meaning than in the real world, and some people collect friends just to demonstrate popularity. Some of these "professional friend collectors" have managed to parlay this into money-making opportunities, including TV shows, but it's my experience that this is getting old for a lot of social network users, who recognize this for the self-promotion scheme that it is. Not that there's anything wrong with self-promotion—I just believe there is a right and wrong way to do it, and again, it comes down to exercising the same rules of etiquette that make for successful social and business relationships in the real world. I also see differences in the way men and women approach the subject of friends on Facebook; men are again more transactional, collecting large numbers of friends in a methodical and unapologetic way as a means to achieve some desired goal. Women, on the other hand, like to focus on people with whom they really do have some kind of social connection, and thus are much more likely to post and share personal photos of their kids and family life.

The answer is to have both a personal profile and a business profile. The process for creating a business profile is the same as for creating a personal profile, but there are a few additional nifty features that can help to promote your business in a professional manner. A business page should be public, which means anyone can see it, and it should include a company logo in place of your personal photo, along with a link to your web site and all the other relevant contact information. Once you've entered the basics of your business page, you can customize it with the additional application functions that Facebook has built in using the "edit page" function. These extras include a discussion board, an event calendar, notes for sharing business news or maybe blog entries, photos, product reviews, videos, and a wall, where, just like on your personal Facebook page, people can leave comments for you, post links, photos, and videos or comment on your status—all for the public to see and read. Once you're done creating your business page, you can then invite all your friends to become "fans" of it. This will automatically keep them updated by e-mail on any new developments you post on your business page, including sales, networking functions, new product reviews and any other special promotions you can come up with.

LinkedIn

LinkedIn (www.linkedin.com) offers a more formal business networking social environment than Facebook. Many people you find on LinkedIn are professionals including attorneys, business consultants, engineers, and academic administrators, who network almost exclusively for business purposes. Many of them will not have Facebook pages or use any other social networks, and they typically represent mid-level to executive talent. There is no shameless "friending" allowed on LinkedIn; instead there are "connections." In order to build your connections, you can invite people you already know to join your LinkedIn network, or you can ask for an introduction to someone you'd like to network with via one of your existing connections who is in that person's network. Once you build your professional profile you can ask your connections for whom you've actually provided goods or services for recommendations of your work, which are posted on your profile for others to see. Just like on Facebook, you can join groups of people who share your interests or expertise, and you can use those connections to build contacts. There are many ways to use additional applications that allow you to build out your profile with additional information including photos and videos. If you provide any professional services that depend on finding, cultivating, and developing a client list, it is imperative that you have a presence on LinkedIn and you work it for all it's worth. Many of my professional friends tell me that this network delivers more business returns than any other network. Still, LinkedIn is finding new ways to compete with Twitter and Facebook by adding new functionalities as well, including a status update question on your profile page asking, "What are you working on?" You can find me on LinkedIn as well under Kim Lavine; stop by and send me a request to join your network.

MySpace

This platform is very similar to Facebook, except that it seems to have a greater appeal to a younger demographic. MySpace has the reputation of being the best place on the Web to promote yourself if you're a musician, and many serious musicians I know have very popular My-Space pages where they sell lots of music to this key demographic. Personally, I don't use MySpace, but that doesn't mean you shouldn't give it a try if you have the time to manage one more social network.

YouTube

You are probably already familiar with YouTube, a video-sharing web site where you can upload, share, and watch videos from around the world on just about every subject in the world. What you might not know is that you can create your own YouTube channel, where you can feature your own videos, connect with more new friends via "subscribers," and find ever more creative ways to promote your message or your business. It's my belief that every web site, whether for personal or business purposes, should now feature all types of media, including videos. If you're selling something, you should make it a point to have a three-minute video commercial promoting the features and benefits of what you're selling, which visitors can watch on demand when visiting your web site. This is easier to do than you think if you have the right video editing software and an ordinary video camera. My choice for software is Adobe Premiere Elements Plus, which you can get for as little as $60 if you're creative and search the Web for bargains. This software is so easy to use, that after reading the short introduction booklet, my 12-year-old son was filming, editing, and uploading his own videos to YouTube, complete with a musical soundtrack and fancy animated titles, without any help from me in a matter of days. Without any promotion, he had hundreds of views from strangers within a week. You even have the ability via the "Insight" tab to track who's viewing your video, including demographics, country, and means of discovery, showing if viewers found it through a viral source, a link, or embedded code on your web site or someone else's. Once you have successfully uploaded your video, you can customize your channel with some of the same features that are available on the social network platforms listed previously, and either post a link to it via the URL, or copy and paste the HTML code for it into your web site management platform to create a mini TV screen view of it on your web page. There are at least a hundred other ways for you to optimize your presence on YouTube, then use that to connect to, inform, entertain, or sell to people all over the world directly or indirectly through links and embedded code on your web site, Facebook page, blog, Twitter page, LinkedIn page, or other social media platform, including my favorite: Ning.

NING

I saved the best for last when it comes to social media platforms. Ning (www.ning.com) was launched in 2005 by Netscape founder Marc Andreessen and Gina Bianchini to compete with MySpace and Facebook, by allowing people to create their own personal social networks around specific interests or communities. You can find my Ning community at www.community.mommymillionaire.com. Made up of members from all over the world, it provides most of the same applications that Facebook and MySpace do and more, while simultaneously offering network creators like me more control. This includes the ability to turn off annoying ads for a fee, as well as to customize domain mapping, to name a couple. In the social media universe, this is where I spend most of my time—giving advice, networking with real friends, reading and contributing to conversations in the forum, posting videos, music, links, sharing comments, participating in real-time chat, making valuable business connections—everything! Another feature that makes this the preferred choice for me when it comes to social networking is that creators have the ability to make it a members-only community, which means you have to submit a quick online bio to be accepted. This feature alone has made all the difference in the world to me and my members, because it has eliminated many of the negative aspects of social networking while preserving the best. As I said before, it's a big world out there and some people are just up to no good. By providing a screening process as a condition of joining our community, we've been able to preserve its integrity by focusing on the features that our members depend upon the most—those that truly create and develop real and meaningful social connections. Unlike many social networks out there, our priority is on our members, not on advertising sales, marketing pitches, head counts, or page views; as a result we've been able to maintain a supportive community, combining both inspiration and practical business advice I believe you can't find anywhere else on the Web. It hasn't been easy to fight the tide of conventional wisdom that has dominated the rapid growth of social media in the last couple of years, which has focused on collecting huge numbers of friends or followers, or even members, then using that contact list to market yourself or your network aggressively without much consideration for any of the niceties of social etiquette in the real world. I decided a long time ago that I was never going to sacrifice the long-term value of my brand or my name for short-term revenues. This would seem to many to be counterintuitive when it comes to business, and it is a decision that has only cost me money in the last few years. But I believe in the end that that is precisely what gives my brand real value, and I'll go to the mat to keep it that way. Besides, I believe some aspects of social media will fall victim to their own success in the next couple of years as the multitude of platforms proliferates and people grow weary of some of the shameless marketing tactics and distracting and endless advertising that we see all around us on the Web, retreating instead to safe, personal communities where people are real.

Not only has Ning been the choice for me in business, but it's also been the best decision for me as a parent. When my son expressed interest in social networking as a creative means to connect and communicate with his friends, I wanted to head off some of the problems that we've all seen that result from exposing your children to millions of strangers on the Web, while simultaneously exerting social pressure on them to accumulate as large a number as possible of those strangers as friends. I let him set up his own members-only community on Ning, which has provided all the same benefits of those other large public networks, like the ability to post photos, videos, make friends, chat, create blog entries, and customize pages, without all the headaches and worry, and most important, without exposing any of the details to the public. I didn't count on it being the incredible learning experience that it turned out to be for him. Exposing children to creative means of expression is like pouring gasoline on a fire—they're already inclined to be creative and haven't yet developed a fear of failing. Before I knew it, my son was creating his own videos—from film to final edit—and writing copy for them that would rival anything coming out of Madison Avenue. I knew a light had been turned on in his head when I heard him say, "My community traffic is falling off; I need to add more content." Next thing I knew he was building skateboard ramps to sell to neighbors, complete with hand cut stencils of his own logo, selling them by pushing them out to the curb with a handwritten "For Sale" sign attached. I saw firsthand how the future for both creative and economic innovation for our country was in the hands of our children, and all we had to do was expose them to the possibility, and they would see opportunities for themselves and others almost immediately that you never even dreamed for them. I didn't set out to specifically teach my son anything about business; he just absorbed it by watching me. He was exposed to the entrepreneurial virus at a young age, when he learned that taking control of one's financial destiny in the New Economy was more about ideas and passion than it was about degrees and job titles. I joke about it now and laugh when I boast about his entrepreneurial spirit, but I also have come to realize with true gratitude and relief that I will likely never have to worry about this child making a way for himself in this world as an adult. He already is possessed of the belief that he can and will do anything he sets out to, provided he works hard, and that reward and money are there for the taking for those who act. Where once I worried about him getting into the best colleges, now I wonder how many companies he'll start before he gets into college. I've even joked that maybe college isn't necessary after all, maybe I'll just drop him off in Newark,

New Jersey, where the state slogan is "Only the Strong Survive," with $10,000—when he graduates from high school, and pick him up in New York city four years later with a first-class education and some undreamed of achievements under his belt. No, I'm only joking, that kid's going to Harvard or MIT—I think.

BLOGGING FOR BUSINESS

Blogging is no longer just for personal use, it's for business. True, almost everyone has a blog nowadays, and as a result I've come to dread the words "new blog post," which flit across my Twitter stream with alarming frequency. Still, blogging is an effective tool for not only creating a meaningful personal connection with consumers or visitors to your web site, it's also a great way to increase your standing in search engine results for free, provided you associate the correct tags or keywords to each entry. Blogging is not necessarily a social media, so I won't spend too much time talking about it here except to point out a few tips that I think are important. If you're going to have a blog, you really should enable people to post comments without moderation, which means without approval by you. Freedom of expression is the cornerstone upon which blogging is founded, so you should respect that by allowing people to freely express their opinions. If someone posts something objectionable, by all means delete it. But if they disagree with you respectfully, I think you have an obligation to leave the post as is. Everybody knows that controversy sells, so a little controversy can create more interest and drive more traffic to your web site. I also have a lot of respect for those people who have the courage to let others publicly disagree with them, and I'm frequently surprised and disappointed when I encounter moderated blogs from the serious press or worse yet, prestigious universities. There are countless blogging platforms out there for you to choose from, with most of them being free. None is perhaps more popular with more plug-ins, or additional free software applications, gadgets, or widgets that interface with the original program than Wordpress (www.wordpress.org).

EMARKETING 101

This is just an overview of the basic tools of social media, which are not only rewriting the way business gets done but also creating a new world culture through the revolutionary ability to communicate in real time with thousands, if not millions of people around the world. Whatever business you're in, you need to start using one or more of these tools to your advantage today. This is a time of epic transformation and epic opportunity; those who adapt and learn to use these new tools first will be the ones who will not only survive but thrive. You can take your chances and ignore them, but they're virtually free to use except for the cost of your time, so why would you? Much of this is do-it-yourself for start-up or even midsize entrepreneurs, though there are so-called experts out there who will charge you tens if not hundreds of thousands of dollars to design and execute an e-marketing campaign. Beware, however, as I'm amazed daily at the number of people who call themselves social media experts who have limited experience with all these tools. It's my experience that you can hire a virtual assistant who specializes in social media to help you execute a social media e-marketing campaign at a fraction of the cost of what some of these supposed experts will charge you. A virtual assistant is an online professional who provides administrative, technical, creative, or social media services for your business at an hourly rate from a location that can be anywhere in the world. According to Frances Palaschuk, founder of Ultimate Biz Assistant, a social media marketing virtual assistant company, an e-marketing plan is designed specifically to market your business online. This can include the traditional components of e-marketing such as search engine optimization (SEO), e-mail marketing, banner advertising, and search engine marketing, most of which cost money, or these new social media tools like blogging, microblogging, and social networking, which target your niche market for essentially no cost other than your time.

MOMS ARE KING

What's becoming clear is that at the same time that advertising is proliferating on the Web, it's simultaneously losing its influence on the consumers that matter. If advertising doesn't work any more, and the opinions of moms do, conversational marketing is the most important marketing you can be doing, with the most important consumers there are: moms. After all, it's commerce that drives everything, and it's social interaction between women that is driving commerce through new product innovation and early-adopting features that the rest of society will eventually adopt. Women are social creatures to whom relationships are critically important. Research shows that most consumers, particularly women, spend over 15 hours a week online, utilizing all these forms of media, so if you want to talk to them, use the same media. But keep in mind that the revolution, influence, power, and promise is not in the medium, it's in the message. Content is still king, and moms are the new kings of content. Forget about Wall Street or even Washington: when it comes to power, women are the new major players, as business owners, consumers, and as social and cultural arbiters in their dominance of this new media, particularly social media.

FREE WEB SITE/BLOG TOOLS/RESOURCES

There are endless resources out there to help you take your social media identity to the next level, and most of them are free. This includes photos, templates, icons, analytics, and design themes, all designed to plug into web sites, blogs, Twitter, Facebook, LinkedIn, and Ning. For an up-to-the-minute list of these free resources, and advice on how to use them to your best advantage, visit www.mommymillionaire.com.

CHAPTER 7

A New Attitude

You think we can do all this without remaking the attitude thing, too? I don't think so!

Not only is there a New Economy, and a new way of communicating, and a new market for products and new channels for distributing them, but there's a new way of thinking in town, and just like in today's economy, you better start reinventing yourself now if you want to succeed.

A NEW WAY OF THINKING

I'm not going to pretend to be an expert on the psychological roadblocks that hold women back from taking their share. I'm just going to speak about personal lessons I've learned from my own experience as a woman on the front lines of business. When I started out, I had no business degree and no business experience. Just like the more than five million people in the United States today who have lost their jobs in the last six months, I was forced to confront tough economic realities to find a way to support my family after my husband lost his job. I was a stay-at-home mom, out of the workforce for five years, with two little boys aged two and four, and a $200,000 mortgage to pay. I started out with a simple little consumer product called the Wuvit® that everyone laughed at, which I managed to take from my kitchen table to the nation's top retailers, racking up millions of dollars in sales, raising private equity, recruiting world-class talent to work for me, designing the first pink ribbon-inspired fabric, creating a lifestyle brand, launching a home décor line, then buying my company back from investors and starting my media company on my own, without any investor money. Along my incredible entrepreneurial journey, I've learned a few things; most important is that attitude is the only thing that separates the winners from the losers. Maintaining the right attitude for success right at the beginning is critical. Unfortunately, I discovered that entrepreneurs—and millionaires—aren't born, they're made, and that the right attitude was a product of the journey and was only arrived at after first confronting then conquering every roadblock I encountered both in my mind and in my experience as a woman in the business world. Some of these roadblocks men experience, too; some of them are unique to women. Here's what I know for sure.

THE SECRET—NOT!

World-famous investor Warren Buffett observed that "You only find out who is swimming naked when the tide goes out." Well, guess what? The credit bubble, which made an abundance of unreal money available to just about anyone who wanted it or visualized it coming to their mailbox for the last 10 years, has burst. The tide has gone out and all those people who were selling you those unrealistic expectations of overnight success without work are the ones who have been swimming naked. The party is over and now it's a time for honesty and all the tough realities that go along with it, time to take the hangover medicine and get back to work. To be honest, I wish I could tell you that this success thing was more about affirmations and forming conscious intentions than it was about working my butt off. It would make me more popular and probably sell a lot more books and make me more money, because everyone knows success sells, and there's no kind of success more in demand than overnight success. But then I would be promoting the same illusions that not only almost resulted in my failure, but were responsible for the failure of 90 percent of the people I've encountered along the way who had million-dollar ideas but gave up on their battle for success without so much as a fight upon their first confrontation with crisis and fear. In my experience, the reason 80 percent of all businesses fail in the first four years, and another 80 percent of those that remain fail in the next four years, is that people gave up when their expectations of overnight success confronted the hard work demanded by reality. Stop the insanity! If I had known that toughness, courage, and action were the key ingredients required to navigate the path to success, I probably wouldn't have been so hard on myself for having to first summon them, then use them without apology as a woman.

NO MORE BANDWIDTH FOR B.S.

Attraction marketers, if you're reading this—move on! Okay, I admit I don't know exactly what attraction marketing is, but I know a lot of people are selling it everywhere I look, and almost all of them haven't sold a thing in their lives, except their attraction marketing services. In the New Economy, there is no more bandwidth for bullshit. It's time for real businesspeople with real business lessons to lead us out of the past and into the future with courage and conviction. That means that if somebody's selling you something that seems too good to be true, it's too good to be true, no matter how desperately you want to believe otherwise. If somebody is trying to sell you business advice, coaching, or consulting services, and has never started or run a business, don't listen to him. It's time to recognize and celebrate all those people who are making money the old-fashioned way: by earning it through hard work, sacrifice, and a willingness to eat risk and sometimes fear for breakfast. These are the heroes we need to listen to and learn from because this is what it really takes to get the job done.

NO TIME FOR SISSIES

It's as if the myth of overnight success has been replaced by the myth of law of attraction success in the last couple of years, no doubt fueled by the overabundance of credit and the pressures it exerted on us all to not only aspire to and have everything, but to make it appear as if we achieved it all, including —homes, cars, and shoes—without effort. I can't tell you how many times I've had to hide or apologize for my hard work over the last couple of years to people who told me I was crazy right to my face. Yes, that's right, I have to apologize for the fact that I work more than 40 hours a week in pursuit of my dreams, which have transformed my life in amazing and powerful ways and opened up unimagined opportunities for me personally and professionally, as well as for my family. After all, these people who were criticizing me had all the trappings of success, including high-paying jobs that didn't require more than 40 hours a week of work, months of vacation each year, cars, motor homes, and vacation properties. They enjoyed these symbols of success while I worked long hours, sticking every dollar I made back into my business, not taking elaborate vacations, and, worst of all, driving an old car! These are some of the same people looking for jobs today. Many of them will be forced to make the same journey I had to embark on five years ago, when my perfect little world came crashing down upon me and I had to find a way to support my family by making sacrifices and taking on short-term risks in favor of long-term reward, while simultaneously creating employment and investment opportunities, which people like them depend on.

IT'S A TIME OF ACTION, NOT THOUGHT

I don't know about you, but I'm tired and worn-out from having to pretend I have built a valuable business without effort or that my life is perfect in every way. Working hard to make dreams come true must be for suckers, given the way our culture has come to justify a weak work ethic. Just look at all these books that tell you how to outsource your entire life, work only hours a week, and think yourself rich. In my experience, the practice of some of these laws of attraction is nothing less than superstition in a new-age guise. Practicing a faith in thought as magic without a commitment to doing whatever it takes when it comes to action to get the job done, is not going to cut it anymore. Pretending that everything is okay when clearly it is not isn't going to work either. Temporarily taking refuge in the "now" might be a good strategy to take the pressure off once in a while, but there is no past or future in the now, so if you don't want a future, spending your time in the now is a good strategy. The same people who espouse this philosophy of thoughts or positive affirmations creating reality in my experience always seem to have a "come to Jesus" moment when it comes to the reality of money and maintaining their fairy tale lives, and I have their e-mailed appeals for money to prove it. Working hard has actually seemed to come to be regarded as a negative trait in this culture over the last couple of years, but now it's wake-up time. It's time to get to work again, America!

SCREW FEAR

Not only has this thinking created an unrealistic image of financial success, it's created an unattainable goal of happiness that we're all expected to somehow achieve. It's as if fear and anxiety are symptomatic of our inability to achieve a desired level of awareness that only people who live in monasteries or perfect temples of denial can master. Since when has it become your American right to be free of anxiety? Since when has it become somebody else's responsibility to give you a job? I know it's tough to hear, but this is America and survival of the fittest is what determines who comes out on top, especially in this New Economy. Thank God we live in the United States, where we have the privilege of competing with no limit to opportunities, talent, education, or even money. Just as in the jungle, fear is good. Fear is an instinct that alerts you to danger that demands your response in the form of action. Fear is a motivator; it's either fight or flight and it better be fight because there's no place to run and hide anymore. Nothing will get you out of bed faster in the morning to do what has to be done than fear. The whole secret to my success may be just having had the courage the first two years to get out of bed and do what had to be done, despite being afraid. In my experience, when I feel anxious, I'm always subconsciously tuning in to that inner voice of mine that is telling me to do something, to rise up, to act—to seize my destiny. I mean, live now, die later!

I'm not talking about irrational fear. You have to learn to live with and manage your fear if you're going to use its energy to drive you on to greater success. I don't know anybody who's rich and successful who hasn't been forced to confront fear and take risks to start their businesses and take control of their financial destinies, often as a result of being fired, downsized, or just becoming sick of doing something they hated. Okay, I admit to knowing a few "lucky sperm club members," people who are rich because they inherited money or successful businesses from their parents. But I personally don't know anybody who has a job that isn't a result of somebody taking a risk and facing fear on a daily basis for years to create that job, usually putting everything they had, including their own family's security, on the line. Successful people know that fear can be conquered by hard work and information, where others allow a lack of information and inaction to create fear. Action is the only cure for fear. That's why you write a business plan—to mitigate the risk and gain control of the fear. That doesn't mean you're not going to be afraid when you begin to execute it. Start by giving yourself permission to be afraid. Nothing is more debilitating than being afraid while having to pretend you're not; don't beat yourself up for being afraid, and don't deny fear. Fear is often change in disguise. We're going to see what people are really made of in the next couple of years, and we need everybody doing their share to take those risks, face those fears, and create those jobs that everybody else needs in order to confront and get over their fear.

SUCCESS IS FOR THE TAKING—NOT THE ASKING

If I had known this at the very beginning, I would have saved myself a lot of agony that came from asking. I have to credit best-selling author Jack Canfield for this revelation. He was leading one of his motivation groups and began it by holding up a $20 bill and asking those in attendance "Who wants this?" Of course, everyone raised their hands. Jack responded by just sitting in silence, looking at the people in the audience who looked back at him, sitting quietly with their hands up. This standoff went on for a couple of minutes, Jack silently holding up the prize, while the group of people sat there wondering what it was going to take to get it. What looked like an impasse was finally broken when one of the group members, tired of sitting on the couch and waiting for something to happen, got up and took the $20 bill out of Jack's hand and sat down with it, putting it in his wallet. That was it. That was the breakthrough moment that he had hoped to illicit. His whole lesson was encapsulated in this one act: Get up and take whatever it is you want.

> The road to success is choked up with people standing in line for permission. So get out of line and go *get it!*

THE "X" FACTOR

Is getting what you want, the achieving of a goal or dream, as simple as giving yourself permission to take it? My experience is that the answer is yes! It's really that simple. Give yourself permission to get what you want, then go after it with confidence. Confidence is the X factor. It's charismatic. It's powerful. It can make people do what you want them to do. It can create powerful belief in your dream by others just by the display of your own unwavering confidence in yourself and it. Confidence is as easy to achieve as putting on a jacket. "Fake it till you make it," should become your mantra. People often say to me, "I could never be as confident as you." Wrong! I don't focus on the past, but the truth is, I'm the product of a totally dysfunctional family upbringing that burdened me with unimaginably difficult challenges, self-esteem issues, and heartbreak at a very young age, the amount of which no person, let alone a child, should have to shoulder in an entire lifetime. I'm not going to talk about that part of my history because there's no profit in living in the past. Believe me, I'm not in denial. On the contrary, I believe my neurotic need for the approval I never got as a child is what pushed me to do the difficult gut-wrenching things that are responsible for my success today. It doesn't mean they were easy. It doesn't mean I didn't beat myself up, or have to overcome fear and self-doubt, or even cry. It's precisely my humanity that I have to thank for my success. But that's not just my story, that's the story of every successful person I've ever met. They weren't confident people for whom everything was easy; they were real human beings with something to prove, some need to redeem themselves, or some unstoppable drive to fix something in themselves that was broken that money just couldn't buy. Don't ask them to tell you what it was. They're always too busy trying to forget about it, or hide it, or bury it. So don't tell me you can't do this. Fake it till you make it by practicing confidence with your head up and shoulders back. As soon as you find yourself lagging, or surrendering to doubt, stop, breathe, smile, tell yourself: "head up, shoulders back," and go on. The truth is, you are all that. You do deserve success and the time for it is now. Count how many times in one day you encounter, and conquer, self-doubt. Understanding that this is nothing but a negative habit that you can correct with one conscious exercise is the first step to you tackling that next challenge of today or of a lifetime.

IT IS PERSONAL—AND IT'S BUSINESS

When I first started out, I thought that if I could eliminate the emotions from doing business, I would have this success thing licked. After all, emotions are messy and personal, and this isn't personal, it's business. I mean, how much easier would it be to make a cold call if I didn't have to worry about hearing "no" for an answer on the other end and feeling hurt? But I've learned that when it comes to doing business, I've come around to a new way of thinking, one that is all about embracing—not denying—the human condition and all the messy emotions that go along with it. Business, after all, is about life, and if you're living your life—I mean really living it—you're on a heroic journey. Most women I meet are starting businesses for all the messy emotions like love and passion that go along with fully embracing their human need to keep family or self-esteem at the center of their lives. They're starting businesses in record numbers, either as a lifestyle choice enabling them to find a way to fulfill personal or professional aspirations without compromising their need to be great moms, or they have a more critical need like trying to escape poverty, attain a dream, leave a bad marriage, or, like me, support their family as the sole breadwinner. Whatever it is, you're lifting yourself up, pushing yourself on, facing down fear, dismissing doubt, and opening yourself up to all kinds of criticism, hurt, pain, joy, love, and success, because there is no courage without vulnerability.

YOU'RE SHIZZNIT, FOSHIZZLE!

That's why I want you to embrace your humanity. I want you to live and celebrate every single moment of every single day of your journey to fulfill your dream, because those moments of the journey—not the money—are the reward. I know as women we're always putting the needs of others before our own, but in this instance I want you to be greedy. I want you to want success. I want you to be unapologetic about wanting more, wanting recognition, wanting fame, and wanting money. I want you to take risks that call on every ounce of courage and faith that you possess to get it, even if it results in pain and disappointment. You are going to make mistakes, that's a given. You're going to confront doubts and fears as well, but I know you're going to conquer them just as I did and as everyone who's ever beaten a path to success has with nothing more than the ability to tell yourself, *"You can do it."* In short—be fully human. Don't try and find success anywhere that doesn't involve confronting life head on with courage, taking risks, and being vulnerable, because it's not there, even though a lot of people are trying to say it is so that they can make money. Acting with courage is hard but it's the only way to live, even if it makes you cry at the end of the day. In the end, nothing of value has ever been accomplished without courage. Everything beautiful, strong, and worthwhile comes from hard work, patience, sometimes even suffering. You need only to look at your children to know that that's true.

HOW SCREWED UP IS TOO SCREWED UP?

The answer is, there is no "too screwed up." I don't care how bad your past or current situation is, there's no embarrassment in it, it's not too late, and there's no limit to the success you can achieve. I've heard so many inspiring stories the last few years in my travels across the United States and Canada from women who transformed impossible situations into incredible success, just with the simple decision to do so. There was the woman in Michigan who told me how she was forced to take a gun pointed at her mother's head out of her father's hands, who after years of beating her, was going to use that day to end her life. She put aside both the anger and the pain that came from living her life in an abusive household and became a successful politician and businesswoman, then took her father in during the last months of his life to care for him before he died through the courage and heroism of forgiveness. Then there was the woman who wrote me to tell me that she had left her own abusive marriage after 25 years after starting her own business gave her the economic means to do so. It didn't mean she wasn't afraid; she was just tired of being afraid and powerless. That's why people start businesses, for all the messy human reasons. Every success has a story like this. One of my favorites is that of Tyler Perry, a Hollywood star with movies, a TV series, and a lineup of successful theater productions to his credit. Besides being a business hero, Tyler Perry is also a testimony to the power of recognizing an underserved niche in the marketplace, and going after that niche, regardless of how much opposition you encounter. There are countless underserved niches in the market ready to be exploited, and only those who are visionary enough to see them, and courageous enough to follow their dreams to reach them, can lead us on to a wider understanding and greater opportunity. But getting there is no easy process for the leader who pushes us to that new frontier. As you'll see from Tyler Perry's story, being a leader often requires enduring hardship, risk, and sacrifice beyond what any of us could anticipate. But as I like to say, there is no reward without risk, and the greater the risk, the greater the reward.

ABUSED *AND* HOMELESS

Perry was raised dirt-poor in New Orleans, where he was reportedly physically abused as a child. He undertook the exercise of writing letters to himself about the anger and pain he suffered as a child as a means to exorcise himself of these negative influences. These letters turned into his first play, *I Know I've Been Saved*. After saving $12,000, he moved to Atlanta for the purpose of staging it. But this isn't a story of overnight success. Perry spent six full years in Atlanta, writing and staging productions, which all failed, leaving him homeless and penniless. At the beginning, unable to afford traditional theaters, Perry staged his productions in unconventional venues like churches that were linked to the black community, referred to as the "chitlin' circuit," and these people, outside of any traditional Hollywood or New York demographic, are what made him. His dedication to this core constituency has not wavered even today. Even though he's become a Hollywood darling, Perry refuses to relinquish one iota of creative control over any of his projects, ensuring that his humorous commentary on this overlooked cultural niche remains true to his vision. It's safe to bet that five years ago, nobody in Hollywood or New York could have been convinced of the financial viability of an abused and homeless man staging acerbic plays about the foibles of a marginalized black community in chitlin' circuit venues. Since then, as of March 2005, Perry's work has reportedly earned him more than $75 million. How many Tyler Perry's are there in the world right now, abused, homeless, pursuing a dream to commercialize a market that doesn't even exist yet? Maybe you're one of them, about to give up on the verge of success, listening to everybody tell you you're crazy and that you're never going to be successful. Don't listen to them! Everybody I know who's ever made it was on the verge of losing it all right before they struck paydirt. As my 12-year-old son puts it: God told Noah to build the ark; he didn't tell him when the flood would come. Build the boat!

WHAT IS SUCCESS, ANYWAY?

And who are they to judge? Is the measure of success sales of a million dollars a year for your company? Or is it staying home to homeschool your child? Is it working in an office at a prestigious company in New York in a 9-to-5 job? Or is it striking out to do what you love with more risk than pay in the hopes of starting your own prestigious company? Is it the person who sells her company for hundreds of millions of dollars? Or is it the person who finds herself burdened with ungodly personal debt to follow some dimly perceived dream of starting that company? The answer is, it's all of these things! Do you think the person who sold her company yesterday for hundreds of millions of dollars didn't take on obscene debt? Do you think she didn't strike out to do what she loved, despite risk and lack of pay, possibly leaving behind a prestigious job with a fancy office? Maybe she squandered an illustrious degree from the country's best university that she earned on full scholarship to stay home and raise her young kids, taking work on the side when she could and accidentally creating a million-dollar business. Or maybe he dropped out of school to the utter disappointment of his parents and started a company in his garage with one computer. Long before Bill Gates became the gold standard of personal entrepreneurial achievement, he wasn't what some people consider a success. Be careful how you measure success, because the measurement of success is changing every day. The book is being rewritten daily as to what the new wealth opportunities of tomorrow are, and only history will judge who is successful.

FOLLOW YOUR DREAMS

The truth is, just as it's easier to find success than it is to find your soul, it's easier to follow money than it is to follow your dream. The dream-followers don't get enough credit in this world. Everywhere you look, there's money and support systems for those who don't dream, whether it's government programs, job-training, unemployment benefits, or bailouts. On the other hand, Wall Street has created its own culture of success on the backs of those dreamers who survived the treacherous hazing that is starting a successful business to create the Wal-Marts and the Hewlett-Packards of this world, where the people who invest in these companies' IPOs are perceived as the heroes, not the people who started them in their garages. When it comes to money, success is relative; Bank of America—which supposedly has some of the smartest financial minds in the business—has a debt to asset ratio of 146:1. I hope that makes you feel a little better about your own financial condition. Many of you who are reading this are among those uncelebrated, unsupported dream-followers, finding their souls and following their vision, taking on personal debt with no promise of a bailout, no unemployment benefits if you fail, unable to afford decent health insurance, forget about pensions. All of you are heroes to me. All of you are successful. All of your stories are success stories.

ARE WE POOR MOM?

I'll never forget the day my son came home and asked me, "Are we poor mom?" At the time he was only seven. "Our neighbors drive a Yukon XL with DVD players in the headrests," he said. "They said we don't drive something like that because we're poor." I couldn't believe the words coming out of his mouth. Though we were living in a brand new 3,000-square-foot house, we drove two aging cars that were obviously attracting the negative attention of my neighbors. At the same time my neighbors were telling my son we were poor, I was putting food on the table for 35 employees. Because of the overabundance of unrealistic credit during the last 10 years, we were all being aggressively marketed debt, but now it's wake-up time. Consequently our whole identification with success in this country has become synonymous with conspicuous consumption, measured by the size of your house and the make of your car and what your neighbors think of them. Conventional wisdom was that if you don't have the biggest and the best, you were obviously not successful. As a result, this country is drowning in consumer debt, with the amount of borrowed funds exceeding 138 percent of household income annually. But those days are over! Just as it takes courage to start a business, it takes courage to drive an old car in this country. It's time to redefine success; it's not about the size of your car, it's about the size of your heart. That's why people who are starting businesses are my heroes. They have the guts to define success on their own terms, while building an asset—their business—possibly worth millions, that their neighbors can't see, touch, or feel. Now that's courage.

SUCCESS IS FREEDOM

Thank God, the pressure is off. What passed for success—a good job, big house, fancy car—just last year is not looking so good to a lot of people right now. You don't have to play that game of keeping up with the Joneses anymore. It's time for the dreamers to take over. You're free to define success on your own terms, and it isn't always about money, it's about freedom. Along my own journey, I've discovered that money ain't all it's cracked up to be anyway. As my mother used to say, "Just because someone has more money than you, doesn't mean they're any happier than you." I've found that money can't buy happiness, and a lack of it can't take happiness away, not when your happiness is measured in love, the ability to spend time with your children, control of your own financial destiny, and freedom.

SCREW FAILURE

If you're going to dream, to give yourself permission to go for it, to push aside fear and doubt on a daily basis to get it while redefining success on your own terms, you'd better learn to say "screw failure," because there is no success without failure. It's not a question of *if* you're going to fail; it's a question of *when*. Failing is easy; getting up again is what's hard. All you need to do is succeed one more time than you fail to become a millionaire. There is no shame in failure. There is only shame in not trying. When it comes to failure, the only thing to fear is fear itself. Be fearless! It takes courage to confront failure and move on; you can be courageous, or you can pack it up, quit, put your tail between your legs, and run off and hide—but I already told you, there's no place left to hide anymore, so obviously that's not a workable option. If you're not failing on a weekly basis, you're not trying hard enough. When you do fail, pick yourself up, dust yourself off and try to figure out why you failed so you can fix it the next time. Learn from your failures and try not to repeat them.

NO SISSIES, NO COWARDS, NO COMPLAINERS, NO QUITTERS, ESPECIALLY NO QUITTERS

Okay, here's where I admit one of my personal shortcomings. I'm a very generous person who will try my best to help everyone who crosses my path to help themselves, but this is where I draw the line. I can't stand quitters. I also can't stand sissies, cowards, or complainers. Depending on what day of the week it is and what mood I'm in, any one of these classifications can make the top of my personal list of things I despise. In my experience, all of these attributes are just excuses people use to avoid confronting their own shortcomings, arrogance, ignorance, or self-defeating attitudes to reach success. How do I know? Because in my own battle for success I've been forced to face my own shortcomings, arrogance, ignorance and self-defeating attitudes, somehow finding the personal resources to rise above them only through the gut-wrenching exercise of courage, ingenuity, and responsibility. I've walked through the fire of failure a thousand times to come out the other side where success waits, and I know the only difference between me and those sissies, criers, complainers, and quitters I meet is their unwillingness to walk through the fire. Do they really expect me to feel sorry for them or help them? I don't think so. In fact, the only path for them to take is through the fire. Nobody can help you make that journey. You're on your own. It's a battle one fights with oneself.

"What matters most is how well you walk through the fire."

—Charles Bukowski

THE CRUCIBLE

That's why people at the top are so unencumbered by all these self-limiting beliefs, because they've already got all that arrogance, ignorance, and self-defeating attitude out of the way. They've confronted failure on epic levels and conquered it, walking where others feared to tread. In my own personal journey I've learned that with every failure I encountered and conquered, I had to call upon newer and deeper personal resources of courage and faith to make it through, simultaneously making me stronger and more resistant to succumbing to future failures. I didn't know that by using every single capacity God has given me to the utmost limit—physical, mental, emotional, and spiritual—that it would make me a more fully realized person every day. I didn't count on getting addicted to the feeling of being a hundred percent alive as I fought off failure and discovered new strengths in myself I never knew I could command. I certainly never expected to find God there.

THERE ARE NO ATHEISTS IN FOXHOLES

If you're going to walk through the valley of the shadow of business, you'd better take God along with you. I'm not going to get into a discussion of what God is. I'll let you figure that out on your own. My faith is very personal and very important to me, and I try to keep it that way. All I know is that if you don't have religion when you start your business, you're going to get religion while you run it, because there are no atheists in foxholes, and if you're running a business, you're spending a lot of time in a foxhole. "Whatever gets you through the night," as John Lennon said, is what I urge you to embrace and celebrate, whatever religion it is or isn't. If you read my first book, you know that I was able to get through the tough times helped by an understanding that everything happens for a reason. In fact, some of the worst things that have ever happened to me have turned out in hindsight to be the best things that ever happened to me. Even the most knowledgeable and worldly cynics in my life have come to see this as an undeniable truth, willing to explain the seemingly fortuitous events simply as "beyond coincidence."

If, like me, you find yourself in the midst of failure, alone, walking through the valley of the shadow of death, have faith that things will work out for the best. Let go of worry and put the outcome in the hands of the higher powers of the universe. If you need to, imagine me there telling you, "It's going to be alright." Things are never as bad as you think they are. Don't listen to anything your mind tells you at three-o'clock in the morning because it's not going to stand the light of day and reason. In fact, the secret to sleeping at night lies in your ability to know that

you've done the best that you can, and the remaining circumstances are beyond your control. If you've done your
best to do everything you can on a day-by-day basis, there
is nothing to be gained by worrying. Give it up to God.
If failure is part of the final equation, accept the failure
and move on. It will be a relief. Failure sometimes is the
greatest gift. It will allow you to put the past behind while
focusing your energy on more productive efforts. Have
faith that if the reward isn't immediately, or even distantly
apparent, it will become so. Learn to see providence in the
little as well as the big events in your daily life and your
life will become filled with unimagined meaning, peace,
and love.

CHAPTER 8

Screw Guilt, and Screw Balance, Too!

If there's an Achilles' heel of vulnerability in the superhero that is being a mom, it's guilt. I've seen women of steel brought to their knees by guilt. I've seen a hundred ways for people and society to make moms feel guilty. It's about time someone said, enough is enough!

SCREW GUILT

Wherever I look I see women suffering from every kind of guilt imaginable under the sun. These are strong, confident, capable, loving women, who are struggling with feelings of inadequacy or failure as mothers and businesswomen, all because they made a decision to dedicate at least a small portion of their lives each day to doing something for themselves, to fulfill their dreams of self-expression, to find reward in starting a business, or to support their families.

YOU ARE NOT A MARTYR

What I'm about to tell you about guilt comes from a first-class understanding and education in it resulting from my years of experience being both a businesswoman and the mother of a special-needs child. *You are not a martyr*. You are entitled to an adult life outside of your role as a mom. You sat in a La-Z-Boy watching endless reruns of *Teletubbies* for 10 hours of nursing every day for three months—you deserve the right to a life, too! Not only are you not a martyr to perfect *mom-ness*, you are not a martyr to perfect housekeeper, perfect beauty, perfect body—you get the picture.

I KNOW ABOUT GUILT

I know there is a rarified place in heaven reserved for any mother of a child with special needs, because we're always battling guilt on an epic level, struggling first with the blame for our children's problems, and then with the unrealistic need to fix them. If only we had done this when we were pregnant. What if we had taken advantage of this resource? What if I hadn't given them that immunization? Maybe if I hadn't let him play so much Game-Cube . . . on and on and on. I'm fighting my own battle on this guilt front on a daily basis, sometimes winning, sometimes not, just doing the best that I can. I see other bright, beautiful women around me doing the same thing, struggling with not only their need to be perfect, but to have perfect kids, too. One of them is the most beautiful woman both inside and out that I have ever met on this earth, who, despite being smart and successful, still finds a way to blame herself for her son's autism. In fact, if there is a cure for autism, it's love and she's the proof. It's so heartbreaking for me to see many of us suffer through this battle, like all battles with ourselves, in silence, internalizing pain and disappointment and letting it stand in the way of our success. I know you're out there, suffering in silence, too, because many of you have reached out to me with your stories. You're not alone. You carry so many burdens that other people will never understand; guilt should not be one of them. It takes a village to educate my son, and it took his school's village of seven educators, during the annual review of his educational needs, to take the burden of guilt off my shoulders as only professionals who are used to dealing with guilt can, assuring me it was his disability that created his daily challenges, and not my failure as a mother.

BACKWARD AND IN HIGH HEELS *AND* UNDERWATER

So when you see us mothers of special-needs children passing by, please smile and lay your coats upon the puddles in our path so that we can walk by a little easier. While most of you are on your way to sporting events, ballet classes, or fun family dinners out in restaurants, we're likely spending our evenings trying to get our children to finish their homework, struggling to keep them mainstreamed in school while feeling overwhelmed with that task on a daily basis. That, or we're pushing them on to their success, advocating for their rights at school, juggling doctors' appointments and behavioral and medication plans, praying for them to develop the confidence to make friends with other kids, while hoping those kids won't reject them because they're different, breaking their hearts as a result and making us feel even more guilty for putting them out there. Please don't judge us or them unfairly; we're doing the best that we can.

YOU'RE NOT PERFECT AND YOU DON'T HAVE TO BE

That's why I can tell you from firsthand experience that saying "no" to guilt begins and ends with saying "no" to perfection. I know it's hard to say no to perfection when we're being sold perfection everywhere we look. From TV commercials to inane supermarket checkout magazines telling you how to have the perfect body and the perfect house, which you keep perfectly clean and perfectly decorated while you bake perfect cookies and serve perfect meals, all in an effort to sell you the products required to maintain perfection. Enough with the unrealistic expectations created by Madison Avenue; not only can you not attain all the perfection you're being sold, you shouldn't even aspire to it. This is what's making millions of women feel inadequate. It's time we took control of the messages being delivered to us in the media and shut down the insecurity factory once and for all. We shouldn't be reading so much about how much we weigh or how beautiful and young we can look or how clean our houses could be, but instead how to start and run successful businesses, how to take control of our financial destinies, how to make money. The messages I want to see are about moms not being defined by the products they consume to conform to this ideal, but by the products they create to define it. Nobody's perfect and nobody can ever be perfect, so stop trying. If you can't achieve perfection, you might as well achieve power, and controlling your own financial destiny is where the real power lies.

BEING IMPERFECT IS WORKING FOR ME

I already told you I'm screwed up, and it's working for me—it can work for you, too. In fact, just the admission that I'm not perfect and you don't have to be either is all some women need to change their lives, and I have hundreds of their personal and written testimonies of that simple fact. One woman wrote to tell me that when she looked at the cover of my first book, she thought, "Oh, yeah. Another mom who's supposedly got it all together." Instead, she was relieved to learn after reading it that I was struggling just as much as everyone else is to keep it all together. When I was first starting out when my kids were two and four, I would jokingly quote Rosanne Barr and tell everyone that, if at the end of the day, my kids were still alive, my job as a mother was done. A spotless house and folded laundry were bonuses my family could only hope for. Now I tell people that my success as a mother is not measured by how clean or well-decorated my house is, but how happy my children are. If that means I have to leave dishes until the morning after making a dozen gourmet caramel apples for my church's fund-raiser, or if I have to look at a pile of laundry that either needs to be washed, folded, or put away every time I come into my house—oh well! Any attempts to try and control it just make me more neurotic than does my acceptance that I can't control it. So the lesson is, don't try to be perfect. Laugh at the laundry, forgive yourself for not being able to get it done, and cry when it seems like it's all you ever do. Some of my best cries have happened while I was ironing. There's nothing like taking the wrinkles out of a bunch of shirts watered by your tears to get some things straight in your head. If I didn't iron and pull weeds, I would definitely be crazy right now. If I have to do housework, as we all do, it helps me to consider with gratitude every article of clothing I have to pick up that my children own that other children may not, every dirty dish or pan I have to wash that served food to them while some children around the world go hungry. It's impossible to be unhappy and grateful at the same time, so if cleaning the house makes you unhappy, exercise gratitude while you're doing it and you'll be ironing those shirts with tears of joy. Before long you'll come to an understanding that everything those pesky kids say, break, or mess up is given to you as a special gift from God to make you laugh, cry, and love in more profound ways every day.

BURN DOWN YOUR HOUSE

If all else fails, resolve to burn down your house and build another one after 10 years, because housework should be the first thing to go when it comes to your list of priorities. This is especially true if you are the parent of young boys like me. Through the years I've seen my kids bring live wild animals, running hoses, skateboards, and screaming friends into the house to build tents with every sheet off every bed as they write secret Indian codes they make up in permanent marker on my walls—usually while I'm on the phone. At first I tried to control the tide of chaos and dirt that followed them, but now I understand that I can always get new carpets but I can't get new kids. I've even given up on running around to straighten up when the occasional neighbor or friend makes an unexpected visit. If they don't like it, tough. I've got an empire to run, here!

SCREW BALANCE, TOO!

The ancient Greeks had this figured out over 2,000 years ago. They knew that balance was just another unattainable ideal built on perfection that human beings could only aspire to and only the gods could achieve. They understood that the truth of all things lies in the middle of two polar opposites and they used this philosophy called The Golden Mean as the founding principle to build one of the greatest civilizations on earth. Why argue with some of the greatest philosophical minds of all times? If it worked for them, it works for me, and it can work for you, too! The polar opposites I try to balance using this philosophy are work and play, with play being defined in my world as time spent exclusively with my kids. Working hard balanced by playing hard suffices for balance in my world, with the majority of the play happening during my kids' summer vacation from school. If my kids aren't sick of the beach or the pool or fishing or skateboarding and begging to go back to school by the time fall rolls around, I've failed as a mother. Fortunately, I do a pretty good job at taking lots of time off to have fun in the summer with my kids; unfortunately I pay for it by working extraordinarily hard the rest of the year. If you happen to catch me during my working hard part of the year, it's not always a pretty picture. My house can be a mess and I can be into my third consecutive day of working without a shower, consoling myself by looking at pictures of all the fun times we had at the beach last summer. I reckon balance not in daily increments, or even weekly increments; I answer to the balance master once a year, adding up the hours spent on each opposite end of the scale and measuring it in my kids' happiness.

EMBRACE THE CHAOS

That's why it distresses me to hear so much talk about "balance" when it comes to measuring women's success in this culture. Everywhere you look, somebody is using it to describe the preferred state of affairs in the life of a mom, holding it up as an ideal and urging us to attain it. Defined as a state of being in which nothing is out of proportion, and all parts of our life are equally emphasized as being valuable and fulfilling, it means that not only are we great moms, but we are also great employees or bosses, great wives, doing our part in our kids' schools, in our churches, and our communities. Whew! I'm tired just thinking of it. Everywhere I go across this great country, women want to know if I have it, and how I got it. My answer is, forget balance, embrace the chaos. Balance is just one more image of unattainable perfection that ultimately demoralizes and oppresses us. Balance is just another guilt trap. If the ultimate goal of achieving balance is to attain happiness in your life, and it's not delivering it—get rid of it!

159

I was shocked to hear that we've been essentially having the same conversation—how to follow our own dreams of personal fulfillment without sacrificing our need to be great moms—for almost 30 years. I discovered this while listening to a keynote speech given by Carol Evans, a woman who has been on the forefront of work and family issues since 1979 when she founded *Working Mother Magazine,* and where she is currently the president and CEO. I understood after hearing some details of Carol's own journey of 35 "no's," when she sought to raise the money necessary to fund her company's growth and development, that it's been a long, hard road that has been paved by a few fearless women, and upon which we're moving forward slowly. I also appreciated her candor when she told the audience that "being an entrepreneur is hard." She didn't try to sugarcoat it, or create another false expectation of overnight success, which would have just demoralized the rest of us on our own entrepreneurial roller-coaster rides of daily ups and downs. Instead of selling us an unrealistic expectation of balance, she described balance as a fleeting, ephemeral experience—like a butterfly alighting on our shoulder, or an elephant at a circus putting first one foot, then two feet, three feet, and finally all four feet on a giant ball just long enough for the audience to gasp and clap, before it fell off. There's your balance!

NO APOLOGIES

So it's obvious that balance comes down to the choices we make as women between our professional lives and our family. For most women, choosing family over profession is a shortcut to a career dead end. As a result, a lot of women I meet are either hiding the fact that they have kids, or apologizing for having to work their lives and schedules around the demands of their kids. Apologizing for having kids is another way of feeling guilty about having them, and that's got to stop right here and right now. Let's get it straight right off the bat: If you own your own business, you don't have to apologize to anybody for putting your kids' needs first; that's the biggest perk of being your own boss. I know it takes a little getting used to, but you'll come around. Of all the problems in this world, children are not one of them. In most cases, they're the solution. If you dropped out of the workplace because you were being penalized for having children, then they should become part of your daily business journey without apology. It was only after some very tough and heartbreaking lessons that I came around to the decision that if I couldn't take my kids with me on my business journey, I wasn't going. Forget about "take your kids to work," this is "make your kids part of your life." For me that means that if I have a meeting with any business professional to whom I'm paying exorbitant amounts of money such as an attorney, and my day care arrangement falls through, I'm taking them with me to that meeting. The same goes for phone calls. I still often work out of my home, where I'm on the phone a lot. Where I used to run into the garage with the cordless phone when a business call came in, or close myself up in whatever bathroom was nearby and available, locking the door while my kids pounded or pleaded on the other side, I now stand my ground and speak over them if I need to. I do believe it's necessary for your kids to learn to respect you and not interrupt when you're speaking, but Mommy's Law says that the minute you get on the phone while at home with children, they will immediately demand your full attention with capricious and unnecessary demands in the most whiny, abrasive voices they can muster. Ignore them, or excuse yourself for a minute, listen and respond to their requests, then get back to business. I can't believe how this simple ground rule transformed my life.

CHILDREN ARE IN REALITY EVIL GENIUSES

Nobody is better at using guilt to manipulate you to get what they want than your own kids. In my experience, this is the hardest guilt to manage. After all, you're already carrying around all this other guilt, it's tempting to just give in to their requests. I'm still struggling with the guilt that comes from working and the resulting temptation to make it up to my kids by buying them things. Sometimes I succeed at holding the line on my dignity and discipline; sometimes I really need a couple of hours of peace to get a big project out the door, even it that means rushing out to buy my kids that new video game they've been nagging me about. That's why I'm giving you a once-a-year pass per child right now to go out and buy that video game or whatever else it is you need to buy to get a couple of hours of uninterrupted work time. They'll still turn out okay—trust me. And you'll have your sanity to keep you company when they go off to college and get married and leave you.

OWN IT!

In fact, I want you to go beyond just not apologizing for being a mom. I want you to own it! After all, there are

38,000,000 women with children in this country, so just from a numbers standpoint, owning your mom-ness makes good business sense. You have a huge market to sell to, which renews itself with each new baby born. There are so many women hiding the fact that they're moms all around me—it's crazy. I can understand having to hide it to get a job. Not that there's anything right about that. If that's what a mom's got to do to support her family, that's what a mom's got to do. In fact, I have dozens of e-mails from women who have sent me their tearful admissions of having to do just that. Once hired, they were worrying if having more children would get them fired. Some of them were single moms who had no one else to count on when their kids got sick and needed someone to stay home with them. I remember my personal shock upon finding out that one of my favorite popular music artists was a mom; she seemed intent on hiding the fact that she had kids. After all, how do you sell promiscuousness when you have a three-year-old at home? I know up-and-coming female recording artists who, despite having paid their dues and attaining incredible honors, are scared that somebody might find out they have kids at home and thus sabotage their pop diva candidacy. It's probably one of the biggest underserved niches out there, and you should be capitalizing on it right now. In fact, that's how Tommy Hilfiger built his empire, selling clothes to a mostly black hip-hop community that up until that point had been marginalized and overlooked by traditional retailers and clothing designers. Maybe someone should have the courage to switch out themes of promiscuousness for lyrics featuring funny and loving commentary about life with children or running businesses, and record those songs instead for the 38 million potential listeners who can relate to that message. But of course, the music industry is going to tell you that nobody wants to hear about moms! I mean, they told Kanye West nobody wanted to hear about God either. They said that rap music was just about sex, drugs, and guns, and they were right about that, weren't they? Wrong!

Let me qualify my admiration of Kanye West. Rap music deserves all the criticism it gets for the objectification of women and all the disrespect that goes along with that, so I'm not going to defend rap music here. But it would be a mistake to throw away all the phenomenal success and undeniable genius of Kanye West just because of this.

Kanye West's music has been called "the new gospel," and it's a title he gladly embraces. When I'm facing some of my toughest days personally or professionally, it's time for me to attend the church of Kanye West. That means queuing up my clean-version Kanye playlist, turning up the volume and letting the bass and beats shake my house from its foundations to the delight of my kids. Number one on that playlist is the song "Jesus Walks," the very song that catapulted Kanye to his superstar success. Besides being an inspirational account of the hero's journey, "Jesus Walks" offers a day in the classroom for the entrepreneur in me. There's a line in the song that says, "you mean if I talk about God, my record won't get played—Huh?!!" Kanye was ahead of his time. He was an innovator. Everyone in the music industry was telling him he could rap about "guns, sex, lies, videotape," but definitely not God because nobody would want to hear it or buy it. He stood up to the entire record industry—long before he was a superstar, when he was still just trying to make it—and stayed true to both his artistic vision and his faith. Now that's courage! Imagine working your whole life to get your one big shot, and putting it all on the line to stay true to yourself. Not only did the song go on to change the music industry and create a music icon, it brought the discussion of faith out of the church on Sunday to the radio airwaves every day for a whole new generation of people who Kanye believed needed to hear the message. I know I did! I still do. Somebody be a hero here and make songs about moms!

> "To be nobody but yourself in a world which is doing its best night and day to make you like everybody else means to fight the hardest battle any human being can fight and never stop fighting."
>
> —E. E. Cummings

MOM THE BRAND

If you haven't figured it out by now, this new revolution is founded on honesty. There's just no more bandwidth for bullshit left anywhere, whether it's business, media, attitude, or brands. The control of the messages we receive on a daily basis that define culture has left the hands of the few and has been put in the hands of the people in epic ways. It's a good thing, too, because this country needs a makeover, stat! We're all in this boat together and we'd better be straight up honest and work together to help each other for not just our sake, but our kids' sakes, as well. At the same time that we're redefining business and media, becoming cultural arbiters in place of cultural consumers, we're also redefining the mom brand. Let's throw out the old mom and make a new one. The new mom is real, not perfect. She's not just an alpha mom, she's not just a rich mom, she's not just driving her kids to soccer in a big SUV while buying shoes in her free time, responsible for dictating only fashion trends. This is about so much more than just shoes—even though shoes are fabulous. The new mom might be married, she might be single and living with extended family. She might be living on Park Avenue, she might be working at Wal-Mart. She might be flying to Paris to buy her wardrobe, she might be sewing original children's fashions at her dining room table and selling them on her web site. She might be a domestic goddess, growing, harvesting, and canning organic foods for her children and living a life of crafts and homeschooling her kids. She might be running a worldwide business, buying the organic foods the other mom is growing while simultaneously supporting the rest of the moms who are opting out and choosing their own lifestyles. She might be leading a top corporation; she might just have been fired for being pregnant. She might have never been uncomfortable a day in her life; she might be homeless. She might have three perfectly healthy children who excel at everything they attempt; she may have a child fighting a battle with cancer, just trying to get to school on a daily basis. The new mom defies definition. She can't be put into a neat little box where she's managed and marketed to. The new mom can be anything she wants to be. So let's stand up for each other. Let's not get in each other's way. Let's see each other's stories and love them all. Let's tear down the old mom brand that limits us and measures us and criticizes us and holds us up to impossible standards that crush us, and replace it with compassion, understanding, and support. Let's tell our stories with honesty. Let's not judge each other. Let's be Manifesto Moms.

166

"Personal truth telling as a path to social change is the most important and enduring legacy."

—Gloria Steinem

MOM VERSUS MOM

Since there is no defined standard against which to measure us anymore, there is no more judging, there is only acceptance. Which brings me to the pink elephant in the middle of the room: women hating on women. Let me make it clear right now: The argument of working mom versus stay-at-home mom is a moot point—next question? That tired, old dog just won't hunt anymore. That discussion went out with the last millennium, and just like every other argument that has come before, it was founded on guilt. If you were a working mom, the implication was that you should feel guilty about compromising your family life; if you were a stay-at-home mom, you were guilty of sacrificing your professional life for your family. Like I said, enough with the guilt already. You're free to define motherhood on whatever terms it is that work for you and your kids, even if that means you travel for your business five days out of the week, or if you haven't been apart from your kids one day in five years—even for school because you homeschool. There are no right or wrong answers, and you don't have to apologize for or explain your decisions to anybody.

WOMEN AS THEIR OWN WORST ENEMY

But this isn't going to be that easy. The ugly truth is that a lot of women are out to get other women at work, at church, at school, in government—everywhere. This is one of the truest and saddest facts of my life. Fortunately, I see this phenomenon going away, dying the painful death it deserves at the hands of women who are instead supporting each other with respect and professionalism. Most of the women I see who are guilty of this kind of behavior are older and/or insecure, and who wants to be that? I don't! The kind of women who sabotage the success of other women at work are often the women who had to battle every kind of barrier put in their way as women to get their own success, and they don't want to see other women get an easy ride. This often meant denying the fact that they were women in order to conform to get ahead, and maybe they're a little bit bitter about that, I don't know. The kind of women that call you bitch behind your back as you pass outside in social settings other than work are threatened by you. Your self-confidence is too big for them. You scare them with your success. Your courage to define yourself by terms outside of the norm is something they're jealous of. They want to keep you in that box where you're easily defined and controlled because anything outside of it makes them uncomfortable and forces them to question their own identities. There's no working with these people. You're bigger than them. As my mother always told me, "Don't dignify their behavior with a response." It's a no-win situation. Don't try to be their friend because they'll never be able to accept you without anger and resentment, which will surface occasionally from behind the friendly persona to hurt you personally or professionally at some point down the line, usually when you're the most vulnerable, because that's the only time they can get to you. Remember you're still a pioneer on the forefront of a new way of living, and people don't like what they don't understand,

and you don't have time to explain it all to them. It's a sad fact that most of the people who will be shooting arrows at your back are women. Besides, if you think they hate you now, wait till you're successful! That's a whole other kind of hate, which is equally applied to both men and women.

THE PINK ELEPHANT

But wait—there's more! It's not just guilt, jealousy, and fear that makes women fight against one another. According to Peggy Klaus, a leadership coach from Berkeley, California, in a January 2009 *New York Times* article titled "A Sisterhood of Workplace Infighting," some women "mistreat one another because of hyperemotionality, leading them to become overly invested in insignificant nuances and causing them to hold grudges." Klaus acknowledges that the same things that give women some advantages, like having a keener radar for other's feelings, allowing them to more successfully manage the personal dynamics involved in the workplace and the world of business, are the same things that can lead to our downfall. "If women take things too personally when challenged or criticized, they are prone to overreaction," she says. Her conclusion is that women have not yet learned to deal with feelings of envy and jealousy in a socially acceptable way, leaving them with unexpressed feelings. There's that old "unexpressed feelings" serpent raising its ugly head again. It's no wonder women haven't learned to deal with their negative emotions in public; we're not allowed to express them in public in a way that isn't directed toward other women, or personally, that isn't directed toward ourselves. We're not allowed to be angry, after all. Our survival depends on going along to get along.

NO MORE BITCHES

In fact, the whole identification of powerful women as bitches has to end. The self-flagellation of powerful women who call themselves bitches has got to end, too. Don't ever let me catch you calling yourself or anyone else a bitch. It's a sign of self-contempt. It shows a lack of respect for the work women are doing to gain legitimate respect in the business world. Maybe I've lost my sense of humor, but I don't think it's funny anymore to call yourself or other women bitches. The bitch is everywhere—the crazy bitch, the dumb bitch, the stupid bitch—and we have to combat it with dignity and self-respect. Most pernicious and omnipresent is the TV bitch, which has practically become an entire entertainment category on its own. In fact, in my experience in Hollywood, casting the bitch is a prerequisite to a large percentage of TV shows, and the women you see on these shows are specifically selected for their bitch factor. They're not real women. There are a lot of real women in Hollywood pretending to be bitches so that they can get jobs on TV. If the bitch drama doesn't exist in a show, they'll create it, often throwing women under the bus and making them compete in ways guaranteed to bring out the claws. This explains why we have bitches in the first place: There is a perceived need to compete against each other for limited success.

THERE'S ENOUGH SUCCESS FOR EVERYONE TO GO AROUND

If you're standing up, you'd better sit down because I'm about to shatter one of the biggest myths there is. In the

New Economy that we're creating, there's enough success for women to go around; we don't have to fight
like bitches for it. It's not easy to get. You're still going
to have to work your butt off for it. You're going to be
taking a lot of people to the mat in your daily nego-
tiations on the path to success, because it's uphill all
the way. People are going to be dropping around you
like flies when the going gets tough. It's going to require stamina to stay the course. It's going to require you
to fight all kinds of battles, calling on every mental and
physical resource you have. Most of those battles will be
fought in your mind. Don't give anybody any ammuni-
tion to use against you. Don't sabotage yourself by stum-
bling upon outmoded and irrelevant definitions of what
kind of behaviors are expected of you. Act with courage,
self-conviction, integrity, and always maintain your dignity.
Hold yourself in the highest regard and demand that others
do, too.

DO NOT GO GENTLE INTO THAT GOOD NIGHT

That doesn't mean you're a pushover. It doesn't mean
you're not tough and savvy and smart and confident when
you treat yourself and others with courtesy and respect.
When you see other women branding your courage and
strength with the bitch word—call them out every time!
Demand the respect you deserve. Fight for what's yours.
To parapharase Winston Churchill, never, never, never
give up. Go to the end not giving up. Fight them in
the boardrooms and the streets. Fight in the schools and
fight in the churches. Fight with growing confidence and
growing strength. Use your backbone to stand up for

yourself and fight. Never surrender, even if you're sub-jugated and starving; carry on the struggle until, in God's good time, the new world we're creating with all its power and might, steps forth to rescue and liberate us from the old.

CHAPTER 9

You're Beautiful

Okay, we're in full-out crisis mode here. I told you before I didn't believe in affirmations as a means to magically produce results, but here's where I make the exception. You're beautiful. I want you to tell yourself that every minute of every day. I want you to tell yourself that in every mirror you look into, in every man's eyes you see yourself reflected, in answer to every magazine cover that stares at you with airbrushed faces photographed under perfect lights and touched up by expensive professionals in Photoshop, as you wait in line at the checkout with your kids, dressed in sweats and wearing no makeup. I want it to be the first thing you feel in the morning and the last thing you remember at night before you fall asleep. I want those words to come rising up out of your subconscious in loud and clear answer to every doubt that ever crosses your mind that tells you that you aren't. I want you to feel your beauty coursing through you when you're doing the dishes. I want you to imagine yourself as Aphrodite in Botticelli's Birth of Venus painting when you're cleaning toilets, rising up out of the waves with toilet brush in hand.

When you're the most tired and anxious, when you haven't taken a shower for days because you've been taking care of kids, when you're working on an impossible deadline, when you're alone, when you're crying, when you're homeless, I want you to hear these words in answer to your tears. I don't care what size you are, how old you are, what color you are, how tall you are, how poor you are, or how successful you are. I want you to *own* your beauty when you walk into a room and *command* your beauty when you talk to people and *celebrate* your beauty when things turned out exactly as you wanted them to, or when things come crashing down around your feet. Unlike any other affirmation you can utter, this one really works, because this one magically produces confidence and confidence is beauty.

THE CRISIS OF CONFIDENCE

Something is definitely wrong that definitely needs to be fixed when 80 percent of U.S. women say they're unhappy with the way they look. That's the startling new statistic from a report by the YWCA, a nonprofit women's organization, published in August 2008 in the *Los Angeles Times*, which concludes that our obsession with a one-size-fits-all definition of beauty in this country has resulted in toxically low levels of self-esteem in both women and young girls. The study also finds that 67 percent of women aged 25 to 45 think they are too fat and are dieting, even though more than half of those same women fall into weight and height categories considered "healthy" by the American Medical Association. As a result, 69 percent of the study's respondents aged 18 and older said they were in favor of plastic surgery as a means to attain the ideally defined beauty, a 7 percent increase over 2006. "We felt the problem had reached such a crisis proportion that we needed to speak up and draw a line in the sand that this must stop," said Nancy Loving, director of communications for YWCA U.S.A. "If you're constantly made to feel inadequate, you're really quite disabled in terms of being able to achieve in other areas of life—academic, social, and political."

"You have to believe in yourself when no one else does. That's what makes you a winner."
—Venus Williams

CONSTANTLY MADE TO FEEL INADEQUATE

How are we going to take over the world if we don't believe we can? How are we going to go out there and take our share of money from private equity investors to start and grow our businesses when we don't think we're attractive enough or we're too fat? How are we going to compete with the men who are getting 96 percent of all the money from angel investors and venture capitalists when we're calling ourselves bitches? Clearly, as I've already proven, there's more than enough money and success to go around. Forget about us for just a minute, and think about what we are teaching our kids, particularly our girls. According to the same YWCA report, 40 percent of newly diagnosed cases of eating disorders are in 15- to 19-year-old girls, with their first symptoms appearing as early as kindergarten. As the constant messages girls and women are getting from the media on TV, in music, on their social networks about what passes for beauty nowadays puts more and more pressure on girls and women to conform to an ideal, it's getting uglier and uglier out there. According to the YWCA study, the mean girls are getting meaner, and bullying based on beauty ideals and social status is on the rise as a result. And girls are taking these same toxic behaviors from the playground to the workplace as they grow up, bringing the bullying with them.

SCREW DIETS

Don't only say no to a one-size-fits-all definition of beauty, say no to this relentless pressure to lose weight and to all the parasitic people in this world who are creating that need through constant media messaging, just so that they can make money selling their inane diet products. I get so many messages to lose weight everyday everywhere I turn, I can't take it anymore. Just say "no" to them in your head, and "no" to them with your wallet. I have a diet and exercise program for you; it's called work your ass off to get rich. Again, it's all about the Benjamins. If it ain't making you money, forget about it! What is important to me, and should be important to you, is exercise, because it gives me energy, self-confidence, and the peace of mind that comes from flooding my brain with endorphins on a daily basis. But I don't do any exercise that isn't fun. The minute exercise becomes just one more chore you have to do to fulfill some Hollywood expectation of the way you're supposed to look, or to make you feel guilty for not doing, it's not helping you. After all, people who have the perfect bodies that you're aspiring to have make a living developing and maintaining those perfect bodies. It's their full-time job to be thin. Most of them probably spend three hours a day in the gym with professional trainers, consulting with a nutritionist and eating well-balanced meals a professional chef cooks for them. If someone wants to pay you a million dollars a year to look like Jennifer Aniston, then by all means, work hard to get a body like that. But if there's no money in it, screw it! Put that energy instead into activities that make you money and don't spend one minute feeling guilty about it! Time is money after all, and I've found that Pilates in my family room before the kids get up delivers the kind of results I used to have to kill myself for, without breaking a sweat and without spending hours in the gym. Confidence is the most attractive thing any woman can put on, and that comes with accepting your body as it is.

DO IT FOR YOU

If you want instant feel good that doesn't involve dieting or sweating, I've got one word: makeup. I want everyone who reads this to go to their local department store and get a free makeup consultation from a salesperson at your favorite cosmetic brand. There is no better instant image makeover and confidence booster than this. You don't need to buy everything the salesperson uses, because that could cost a fortune. Buy the one or two things that make you feel good. Even when I'm tired, makeup can make me feel like a million bucks. I've been in some of the best studio makeup chairs in the business, and using the few tricks I learned from my one makeover by a Mac Cosmetics sales associate is all it takes for them to tell me that my makeup looks perfect, even though I don't spend more than five minutes on it every morning. If you already feel beautiful without makeup, then you don't need it at all.

I just use it as a tool, like all the other tools I have in my toolbox. Just like everything else, your beauty and your confidence do not have a be-all and end-all in make up. Don't aspire to the same images of beauty that they're trying to sell you. Those women don't look like that in person either. Take what works for you and leave the rest. As for me, even though I spend a lot of my time working out of my home, I've learned it's important to me to dress every day as if I'm going to an office—in my office we wear jeans to work every day—including makeup. It's just a fact that it has a big impact on my attitude throughout the day. I'm not doing it for anyone else—I'm doing it for me.

SCREW AGE

It's no wonder we're all falling apart when we turn 40 in this culture, when our whole worth as women is measured by how we look. Screw age, too! I've found that after the age of 27, everyone is pretty much the same age anyway. I've met 20-year-olds with more experience and more beautiful minds, rich with thoughts and ideas and questions, than a lot of 60-year-olds. I have 60-year-old friends who are younger by far than a lot of those 20-year-olds, if you measure youth in intellectual curiosity, fearlessness, and passion. I don't care how old you are, it's not too late to get started turning your dreams into reality, to start a business, to have children, to write a book, to have a career in TV—to change your life! Forget about your age and focus on your passion. Passion is what makes people young and beautiful and attractive. Find your passion and

pour gasoline on it and let the fire burn down any pre-
conceived notions you have about your age and anyone
else's age, then turn it loose on the world and see what
incredible journeys it has yet to take you on.

PASSION IS SEXY

When passion walks in the room, everyone stands up. Passion is the spark that lights the gasoline that is life. Passion
is what everyone wants and if you have it, people will
either want to be like you or be with you. In a meeting or
a party or in any group, the people with passion in their
eyes are the people whom everyone else is listening to and
watching. They're the leaders. Everyone looks to passionate people for what's next, because their passion leads us
to horizons few have the vision or the courage to explore.
People are not born passionate. Passion is the process by
which you manifest your dreams, and far too many people
in this world have given up on their dreams or sacrificed
them for a comfortable way of life or a secure job. That's
why passionate people rule; they're making their dreams
happen. Entrepreneurs are passionate people. They're not
content to sit around and let life happen to them; they're in
control of making life happen. That's why some people in
this world are jealous of passionate people. We're taught
early to go to school, get good grades, get a good degree,
then a good job with a good title in a good career track.
Becoming an entrepreneur means learning to value ideas
and passion over degrees and job titles. Entrepreneurs are
working outside of the box, outside of the system. They're
taking risks most people only dream of. They're using their
brains and their hearts and their vision to become more

realized people every day. People running on passion are 100 percent alive, using every single capacity God has given them to live life to the limit on the physical, mental, emotional and spiritual spectrum every day. No wonder some people are jealous of passionate people. You don't need those people.

SMART IS SEXY

Instead of worshipping thin and cookie-cutter beautiful women, I wish the media would just for once show women who are valued for their smarts and talent. I'm qualifying this statement by saying you're already beautiful, regardless of how close you come to the standard of beauty defined in our culture by the media. But I want women to go to Hollywood not worrying about how beautiful they are, how thin they are, how young they are, but instead how smart they are. I want them to watch TV from their couches in their homes and not feel intimidated or inadequate by the endless close-ups of flawlessly beautiful women with perfect skin selling them age-defying products, effectively delivering the message that if these beautiful women aren't beautiful enough, and young enough, and confident enough to be happy with themselves, how can you be happy with yourself? I wish, instead, we could see these women's brains in action, because smart is sexy and nothing is more attractive than intelligence put together with confidence. That's an unstoppable force of an illimitable scope. If women are going to compete with each other, I want them to compete to see who's smarter—not in an academic sense—I'm talking about developing modern-day Renaissance women.

RENAISSANCE MOMS

A Renaissance man or woman is defined as a person who has wide interests and is expert in several areas. Leonardo Da Vinci was the original Renaissance man, capable of painting, writing, sculpting, inventing, and accomplishing learned feats in science. I want to see us smash every pre-conceived notion of what a mom is; break out of every narrowly defined category they can put us in to keep us in our place; transcend every demographic of age, weight, color, economic class, or education level they use to sell us products; redefining our success with new messages and taking those messages across the world. I want to see a renaissance of Renaissance women. I want you to read poetry when you're in love. I want you to find strength openly celebrating your faith. I want you to cook with abandon and bring flowers forth on the earth in your gardens that will fill the world with butterflies and birds. I want you to get intoxicated on creating beauty in your homes and in the products you design to make the world a more beautiful place. I want you to create businesses that will change the way people do business. I want you to shower the people you love in life with love, becoming more and more beautiful with the more and more love you become. There is nothing so beautiful as love, so be love. Look for your beauty in love, not in the mirror. I want to see beauty judged not just by what you're thinking but by the amount of love you're creating. I want you to use love to make, feel, and see yourself as beautiful every minute of every day. I want to feel your love coming before you enter the room. I not only want you to use love to transform yourself but to transform the world.

CHAPTER 10

The 100 Percent Solution: How to Start a Business for $500

The beginning of all equality for women starts with the ability to make money. Now that you have the tools, the knowledge, the lifestyle manifesto, and the power, use it to create the change—and freedom—you want in your life. Whatever setbacks, roadblocks, or even jerks you're dealing with, taking control of your financial destiny is the first step to solving all the personal issues you thought were your fault, or that you deserved, or that you could not escape. Money will get you out of all them, including bad marriages, bad jobs, bad educations, and just plain old bad. Good-bye bad!

LET'S GET THIS NEW ECONOMY PARTY STARTED!

Tell all those people who are telling you that you can't do this the same thing I told all those people in my life who told me I couldn't do this: Your underestimation of me is what drives me on to greater success every day. Invite yourself to the New Economy party, where exponential growth equals exponential opportunity. All you need is $500 and a spirit of innovation. The people taking the risks right now are the people who are going to cash in on the big rewards just down the line. Forget about brass balls, let's use brass boobs to start our own companies, make our own movies, create our own hedge funds, start our own corporations and do whatever we want to do.

FIRST THE UNITED STATES, THEN THE WORLD

Don't look for success where everyone else is looking for it, look where nobody else would think to look. There is opportunity all around you to take control of your financial destiny—you just need to learn to see it. Opportunity is there in the midst of all the day's mundane moments. Once you train yourself to see it, you'll see it a dozen times over each week. Entrepreneurs know that there is never a shortage of ideas, opportunities, work, or even sales; the only limit to how much success you want is how hard you want to work. Success is for the taking, not for the lucky. In fact, there is no such thing as luck. Luck is preparation meeting opportunity. Successful people first had a vision, then they positioned themselves to be on the receiving end of opportunity. This includes homeless, abused, frightened,

183

poor, marginalized, disenfranchised, and minority people; in other words, no excuses, no crybabies, no quitters, and definitely no complainers. Finding opportunity is easy; acting upon it is what's hard. Having the courage to act upon opportunity is what separates those who succeed from those who fail. Learn to see opportunity all around you to make the world a better, or prettier, or kinder, or easier place and have the courage and the passion to face the challenge and get it done. It's a time of great possibility, and you can be part of it!

IT'S ALL ABOUT THE BENJAMINS

You want to start a business but you can't get past your fear of taking the risk and striking out. Reduce the risk, and you may find taking that first step easier than you ever imagined. If you're willing to invest $500 and some of your time, following these steps below may get you to where you want to go faster than you ever thought possible.

Business Model: No business is easier to start and requires less capital to operate than a service business. This is a business that utilizes your time and expertise to generate revenue. If you have professional skills, like bookkeeping, graphic design, or a talent for home-organizing, you can start as soon as tomorrow selling your time and expertise for a premium. People are busier than ever and willing to pay for services today that just yesterday they would have done themselves, so be creative!

Business Plan: Once you've selected the service you want to sell, visit SCORE (www.SCORE.org) or your local Small Business Development Center (www.sba/SBDC.gov)

and get the free help you need to write your business plan. They'll also help you comply with all the government registrations on the local, state, and national level, which, for the most part, cost nothing. Here's where you'll come up with the name of your company and its logo; remember, you sell to a consumer's heart—not her head—so be original. Search your company's proposed name at the United States Patent and Trademark Office at www.uspto.gov and see if it's available to register as a trademark, which currently costs $328. If your business takes off, you could franchise the concept and make millions—think Geek Squad—provided you have strong intellectual property.

Web site: You don't need a brick-and-mortar storefront anymore to start a successful business—all you need is a web site. You can find many easy-to-use services on the Web that can get you up and running like Go Daddy.com's Website Tonight (www.godadday.com) for as little as $4 a month. You can register your domain name there, too, for as little as $7. Most web site building tools don't even require that you know HTML anymore—it's all point and click!

Marketing: You can easily get your name out into the marketplace for free by writing a clever press release and sending it out to local media. You can learn how to write a good press release and even post it on the Web to be distributed to media across the country for as little as $40 at PRWeb (www.prweb.com). Having a good story is what's going to get you media attention, and as long as you focus on a human interest angle that will captivate and inspire the reading public, you'll get noticed. Network by joining local service clubs, or maybe start a blog at Wordpress (www.wordpress.com), to get your unique point of view and helpful tips out there.

Sales: In all my years in business I've never spent any money on advertising except for trade show directories, which went out to hundreds of thousands of wholesale buyers across the country. In fact, I've opened most of my accounts, and some of the nation's biggest retailers, using cold calls. This is easier than you think, and it is detailed in my book *Mommy Millionaire*. For now, you just need to remember three things: Introduce Yourself, Show Them the Money, and Ask for The Sale. These three things are the essence of an "elevator pitch," and can be adapted for the e-mail pitch, voice mail pitch, and trade show pitch. It should never take you longer than 30 seconds to give your elevator pitch, and it should include your name, the name of your business and/or product, why the person on the other end of the line should be interested, including any relevant sales data or potential market or features. Most important, it should conclude with a call to action, whatever that happens to be for you. Do you want the person's address so you can send samples? Do you want a meeting? Can you e-mail some information? What is the most direct path to the money? After cold calls, the only other thing that has resulted in real sales for me is grassroots marketing involving face-to-face interaction with the customer or client. Both of these things are free, so get busy making sales and don't be tempted to spend money on consultants, or advertising, or sales reps, because passion sells, and nobody is more passionate than you.

Making the Money: You will no doubt start bringing in revenues and you need to accurately track and account for those revenues for tax purposes. The gold-standard accounting program is QuickBooks. Setting up QuickBooks for a service business is easy. You can buy QuickBooks Simple Start online at www.amazon.com for anywhere from $40 to $90, depending on whether you're willing to buy it used. Not only will you be able to capably handle the financial functions of running a successful company, but QuickBooks will make you look like a pro doing it, producing invoices and job quotes to present to your customers.

For more information on how to start or run a successful business, visit www.mommymillionaire.com, where you'll find invaluable resources including where to find start-up capital, to help you turn your dream of financial independence into reality.

CHAPTER 11

Complete and Total World Domination

I talked about the money, now let me talk about the love. This isn't just an economic revolution, or a communication revolution, or a family revolution; this is a love revolution.

A REVOLUTION OF LOVE

Women aren't remaking every cultural institution in the United States and the world for money—they're remaking them for love. Love for their children and their families is what is at the eye of the hurricane that is leveling all the old and outdated and pretentious thinking that brought us to this epic turning point. Love is not only the force that is holding the stars apart, it's the force that is healing our wounds, providing us with hope, feeding our children, cleaning up the messes, ending wars, and creating a new economic sustainability not just for our country, but the world. Love is the power of the sun burning off all the greed and illusion that has made us slaves to image while crushing our spirits, and a vast remaking of the human psyche is under way, freeing us all from chains and instituting a new world order.

TOUGH LOVE

Some of these lessons are going to be difficult for some. But everything beautiful, strong, and worthwhile comes out of intense work, patience, time, sometimes even painful suffering. Don't let anybody tell you anything different; they'd be lying or they'd be deluding themselves. How well you walk through the fire will determine how much better, smarter, and more beautiful the person is who comes out the other end. The same conditions that brought this economy to its knees are the same things that are going to drive innovation, creativity, and economic rebirth, not just for our benefit, but for the benefit of the world. Once we face reality and take a tough look at ourselves and the ideals we've built meaning around the last few decades, we're going to be relieved to let them go. We're going to sweat them out like a bad sickness, and after that the clouds will part, the sun will come out on a new, bright, sunny day, and we'll all be able to see the future more clearly. We'll know what needs to be done, and we'll have all the tools and knowledge and confidence necessary to do it.

LOVE THYSELF

Surely the first lesson for women is to love ourselves. We can't take our place as thought leaders in the new world order until we eliminate all the self-doubts that are holding us back. Practice unconditional love for yourself to first recognize and then get rid of the fear, guilt, doubt, and feelings of inadequacy that are taking up too much space in your mind. Call out those negative messages that are entering your consciousness each day, and replace them with positive, empowering thoughts about how beautiful and capable and deserving and valuable you are, not only on a daily basis, but a minute-by-minute basis. Get rid of the unfulfilling relationships, jobs, or ideals that aren't leading you to success or money, even if some of those relationships, jobs, or ideals are the ones you hold the closest. Take out the trash, and once you've done that, guard your heart and thoughts and mind from negative influences with fierce resolve. Computer programmers have a mantra: garbage in, garbage out, meaning if you program in faulty code or negative behaviors, you're going to get faulty and negative results. You're precious; root out and eliminate all the negative code, then reprogram yourself to keep it precious, holding yourself in the highest esteem and showering yourself with unconditional love.

SHARE THE LOVE

Once you end those negative relationships, know that you are not alone. You don't have to be alone, anymore. You can't make it on your own, especially if you're going to commit to be a leader. It's just too hard. You have community; it just might not be the family, friends, or neighbors that you thought. Seek out the community on-line at www.mommymillionaire.com, where there are people just like you redefining success, following their dreams, creating the New Economy while focusing on family and sustainability. Many of you have supportive family and spouses around you as you commit to this heroic journey, but I know many more of you do not. The only people who can really hurt you are the ones you love the most. Sometimes, looking to family and friends for the support and encouragement you need to successfully navigate this journey can set you up for heartbreak. I learned a long time ago not to expect my family or even a lot of my friends to understand my unique journey. My strategy for dealing with this is just to not talk about my work and instead talk about theirs. In the meantime, seek out and surround yourself with the kind of people you want to be like, people with whom you can talk openly and honestly, people who can provide you with the support and inspiration you need to get through each day's battle to be true to yourself and to turn your dreams into reality.

REAL LOVE

In the new world order, it's no longer about acquiring things; it's about being real. It's not about the individual; it's about the community. It's not about a few people getting ungodly rich; it's about creating economic sustainability for the many. Everything has to be scrutinized and passed through the bullshit detector to eliminate all the unreal images of success and happiness that people are always trying to sell you. What's important now is honesty,

191

and integrity. We have to stop focusing on appearances and start focusing on what lies beneath, the real heart and soul and trials and tribulations and loves and laughter of human beings. Love is most genuinely found in human relationships and that's where we need to focus all our energies. Real human relationships and real love must be the engine that drives the New Economy and the powerful tools of social media. I already see evidence of people using these tools in a disingenuous way to continue selling us all the needs of the insecurity market, and we can't let that happen. Some of these people are women working undercover for the male-dominated advertising agencies, and what have they done for us lately? This is our opportunity, this is our communication revolution, this is our media and our message and our $8.5 trillion market to spend on our businesses—get in line behind us! We're trying to save the world here—not just make a buck. If you're not part of the revolution, you're part of the problem. If you're not for us, you're against us. Whoever does not know love, will not know success.

ABUNDANT LOVE

When success is measured in sustainability, there's enough success for everyone to go around. That means buy mom and buy local and buy green and buy handmade and buy American and buy anything from anyone who has a vision for the future and has committed every resource they have to making it happen every day for themselves, their families, and for the global community. The economic reality is that we simply can't continue to breed creativity and innovation, especially when it comes to consumer products, and sit by and watch big retailers and big corporations apply mercenary tactics to scout out those innovators and knock them off. Small business just can't compete with these big corporations anymore, which have means and money and production values with such vast economies of scale that they can take every new idea that is breathed into life and replicate it in numbers and at costs that exhausts me with feelings of helplessness and leaves the creators broke and bitter. This consumer economy we've created is cannibalizing itself. Record trade deficits prove that it's a failed business model and the end is near. We're not fooling around anymore when this country loses five million jobs in just months. We have to find a way to create and support five million entrepreneurs now because those jobs are not coming back anytime soon, and because women appear to be the ones who are the most willing to step up and get the job done, you'd better buy from women, sell to women, hire women, promote women, celebrate women, recognize women, and love women.

HEALING LOVE

If you're lost and lonely, I want you to feel love. If you're broken, bitter, and defeated, I want you to lift yourself up with love. If you're homeless with children, I want you to know God's love and take it with you on your journey to protect you and sustain you and renew you with a vision of faith in the future that your children can see written across your face. If you're scared, I want you to surrender to love. When you enter the valley of the shadow of death, follow the path of love and you will never take the wrong step nor will you ever be alone. Love will always lead you to the light. Take care of the love, and everything will take care of itself. Have faith in love. The secret is in the power of love. Love is the doorway between body and spirit, so keep it open and don't block up the way.

Now go rock the world. Tell them I sent you.

Afterword

I hope all of your journeys will be as exciting, demanding, rewarding, challenging, touching, and enriching as your dreams.

I hope you push yourself to your limit, learn things you never imagined, confront fear with courage, stand up to those who underestimate or dismiss you, go places and do things you never thought you could.

I hope you discover newfound freedom and happiness that isn't so much about the money as it is about the dream and the journey to achieve it.

I hope you take every opportunity possible to look deep into your children's eyes to tell them that you love them, with an understanding that everything they do, say, mess up, or break, is given to you as a special gift from God to make you laugh, cry, and love in new and more profound ways every day.

I hope you cry a little; I hope you laugh a lot.

I hope you take time to recognize and thank everyone who contributes to your success.

I hope you sense God looking over your shoulder at those difficult times when you want to give up, reassuring you through faith that everything happens for a reason.

I hope you love yourself and others with a passion that isn't afraid to be vulnerable or to take risks.

I hope you are a positive, big picture person, always striving to work for the highest good of all parties.

I hope you act with integrity at all times, especially when it is more difficult to do so.

I hope you can look back on your journey and be proud of all the things you accomplished.

Kim Lavine
June 2009
www.mommymillionaire.com

About the Author

Kim Lavine is the best-selling author of *Mommy Millionaire*, president of Mommy Millionaire Media—a multimedia company focused on developing traditional and new media opportunities in publishing, TV, radio, social networking, and digital formats—and of Green Daisy—a lifestyle brand focused on balancing life with love™. Identified as America's expert on inspirational business advice, Kim has appeared on *The Today Show*, *Rachel Ray*, NBC and ABC news, CNN, CNBC, FOX, NPR, Oprah & Friends Radio Network, and LifetimeTV.com. She has been featured in *USA Today*, *Country Living*, *Guideposts*, *Women's World*, and *American Baby*, to name a few. Kim is on a mission to empower people to follow their dreams, inspiring them with hope, honesty, and faith.

Watch Kim's Media Highlights at http://tinyurl.com/mommy-millionairemediahighlight.

"Everything begins with a search for something better—
a dream, an idea, the courage to face a challenge,
and the passion to get it done.
You can do it.
Believe in yourself.
Change the rules.
Join the revolution."

From *Mommy Millionaire*, by Kim Lavine.

Index